"Carolyn Castleberry gives us informatio of investing seem simple and easy to under[...] in broadcast journalism and Christianity p[...]w from which to launch her proven theory[...]

—JULIE JENNEY
Managing producer, *Living the Life*

"Carolyn Castleberry has given us an important work that will ultimately prove indispensable for most women. She has taken a timely idea and turned it into a book that is challenging, engaging, lively, and, above all, enlightening."

—HERB COHEN
Author of *You Can Negotiate Anything* and *Negotiate This!*

"Carolyn Castleberry captures your heart and imagination with her account of [the Proverbs 31 woman whom she calls] Proven. She challenges you to apply the wisdom of Proven and watch God transform your talents into your best life now. A must read for anyone who desires to find significance in life."

—KELLY WRIGHT
National network correspondent

"Managing money has always intimidated me. I feel wholly inadequate and unprepared. Yet, deep in my heart, I would truly like to accept the challenge. This book has both encouraged and equipped me to begin the journey. Thanks, Carolyn."

—TERRY MEEUWSEN
Cohost, *The 700 Club*

"As a woman in the twenty-first century, it is wonderful to know God has not forsaken us. Carolyn has written a book that will encourage you to 'be strong and courageous.' God has always had His love and favor on women, and after reading this book you'll be more comfortable taking charge of your money. When we understand our role from God's perspective, we become liberated to fulfill our purpose."

—ANNE BEILER
Founder and CEO of Auntie Anne's, Inc.

"Timeless advice for today's woman from a successful entrepreneur with a proven track record. *Women, Take Charge of Your Money* encourages women to use their God-given resources and creativity so they will have meaningful, prosperous lives. Carolyn takes a fresh approach in motivating women to meet with their 'real boss' and follow His direction for a rewarding and successful career."

—PAT ROBERTSON
Chairman and CEO of the Christian Broadcasting Network, Inc.

"In my counseling practice over the years, I have seen so many times where disaster could have been avoided if women had done the things Carolyn advises in this book. God never said for you to be either passive or in the dark about money. Read this and get busy. You will be glad you did."

—DR. HENRY CLOUD
Bestselling author of the Gold Medallion Award-winning *Boundaries*

"Looking for direction in your life spiritually and financially? This book is for you. I have been a CPA for eighteen years and have found there are very few books that explain investing in a way that is so clear and easy to understand. This book made a difference in my life and it will do the same for you."

—KIM PAINTER
Certified public accountant

WOMEN, TAKE CHARGE OF YOUR MONEY

A BIBLICAL PATH TO FINANCIAL SECURITY

CAROLYN CASTLEBERRY, M.A.

Multnomah® Publishers *Sisters, Oregon*

WOMEN, TAKE CHARGE OF YOUR MONEY
published by Multnomah Publishers, Inc.
Published in association with Ambassador Literary Agency, Nashville, TN

© 2006 by Carolyn Castleberry

International Standard Book Number: 1-59052-662-7

Cover photo by Wade Studios
Interior design and typeset by Katherine Lloyd, The DESK

Italics in Scripture quotations reflect the author's emphasis.

Unless otherwise indicated, Scripture quotations are from:
New American Standard Bible © 1960, 1977, 1995 by the Lockman Foundation. Used by permission.

Other Scripture quotations are from:
The Holy Bible, New International Version (NIV) © 1973, 1984
by International Bible Society, used by permission of Zondervan Publishing House
The Holy Bible, New International Reader's Version (NIrV) © 1995, 1996, 1998
by International Bible Society, used by permission of Zondervan Publishing House
The New Life Version (NLV) © Christian Literature International, 1969
Holy Bible, New Living Translation (NLT) © 1996.
Used by permission of Tyndale House Publishers, Inc. All rights reserved.
The Holy Bible, New King James Version (NKJV) © 1984 by Thomas Nelson, Inc.
Contemporary English Version (CEV) © 1995 by American Bible Society
The Amplified Bible (AMP) © 1965, 1987 by Zondervan Publishing House.
The Living Bible (TLB) © 1971. Used by permission of Tyndale House Publishers, Inc. All rights reserved.
The Good News Bible: The Bible in Today's English Version (TEV) © 1976 by American Bible Society
The Holy Bible, New Century Version (NCV) © 1987, 1988, 1991 by Word Publishing. Used by permission.
The Message © 1993, 1994, 1995, 1996, 2000, 2001, 2002 Used by permission of NavPress Publishing Group

Multnomah is a trademark of Multnomah Publishers, Inc., and is registered in the U.S. Patent
and Trademark Office. The colophon is a trademark of Multnomah Publishers, Inc.

Printed in the United States of America

For information:
MULTNOMAH PUBLISHERS, INC.
601 N. LARCH • SISTERS, OREGON 97759

Library of Congress Cataloging-in-Publication Data
Castleberry, Carolyn.
Women, take charge of your money / Carolyn Castleberry.
    p. cm.
Includes bibliographical references.
ISBN 1-59052-662-7
1. Women--Finance, Personal. 2. Women--Religious life. I. Title.
HG179.C355 2006
332.0240082--dc22
                                                                    2006001481

06 07 08 09 10 11—10 9 8 7 6 5 4 3 2 1 0

For Lindsay and Brooke,
my beautiful daughters and
Proverbs 31 investors in training.

Contents

PART III—INVEST

PART IV—PROVERBS 31 PURPOSE

ADDITIONAL HELP

Where All This Started for Me

For most women, reading Proverbs 31 and the never-ending list of female virtues recorded there probably produces a mental response along these lines: *You've got to be kidding! She "plants a vineyard"? She provides food for her "maidens"? Who has maidens nowadays? Who does this lady think she is, making the rest of us look bad?*

If you've reacted that way to this passage, then trust me, you're not alone. I responded the same way when I first read this woman's list of seemingly impossible feats. But I've come to believe that the person portrayed in these verses is a God-given model to lead us on the path to financial freedom and a well-balanced life (which is why I've included the entire passage at the end of this introduction).

When I first read Proverbs 31 as a younger woman, I couldn't relate at all to this person. I thought she was a machine, thoroughly unrealistic and irrelevant to our modern world. "She rises while it is still night"? Come on, who does that?

Well…as I came to find out, most mothers of this world

get up while it's still dark outside. What mother hasn't gently nudged her slumbering husband when the baby cries in the middle of the night, only to be met with increasingly full-mouthed, thunderous snores? (By the way, I think they fake this deep sleep. No one can be that comatose.)

I also couldn't understand the part about considering a field and buying it. Who buys fields?

Surprise! Now *I* do. Okay, not quite fields, but income-producing real estate. After many mistakes, much consideration, years of education, and patient trust in God, I found that this method of investment gave me the freedom and resources to walk away from my former job and to search for more meaningful work—slowly and deliberately. And if *you* ever hope to be free financially, then just like the Proverbs 31 woman, you have to do *more*. More than just a savings plan. More than just burying your money in the sand and hoping it grows on its own.

In this irritatingly perfect woman, God has given us the perfect money model, and one that's always current.

(Use these wide margins to jot down your reflections, your questions, and especially your responses to the "Application Actions" scattered throughout this book.)

MY OWN JOURNEY

My own financial journey actually began on the day I realized, as a first-time mother, that I didn't know anything about money. I was holding my newborn daughter in my arms, and the reality hit me that I didn't have a choice to stay home from work and raise this baby girl myself. The issue wasn't reaching my highest potential through the workplace or finding my destiny through a career. The issue was, plain and simple, money—we didn't have enough. As a struggling young couple in a volatile industry (broadcasting), my husband and I hadn't realized the numerous financial choices that actually had always been there for us.

Here's the thing: I was supposed to be an expert in financial matters. At least I looked that way on paper. A few years after graduating with degrees in business and journalism, I'd landed a job hosting a national radio show called "Women Talk Business" on the Business Radio Network in Colorado Springs. I continued my broadcasting career in local television news in Virginia, where I covered many financial stories. But the school of hard knocks would be a much more capable teacher of what actually works and what doesn't concerning money.

I wasn't alone in my lack of financial know-how. In two decades of broadcasting, I've also met some of the brightest, toughest, and seemingly most enlightened women, many of whom don't know how to balance their checkbooks. One day I was in the makeup room chatting with a female reporter about investing. (Yes, I actually did talk about this stuff with my coworkers, much to their discomfort.) This lady had a reputation as a street-wise investigative reporter, and I was stunned when her hard shell dissolved as she admitted she didn't know anything about investing—though she quickly regained her composure by pretending she really didn't care. I asked her how she ever planned to retire. Her answer was straight from the dark ages: "I plan to marry a rich man, of course."

A degree or a job doesn't guarantee financial success or freedom.

A job, any job, doesn't guarantee financial success or freedom. Though television personalities seem to have really cool gigs, it's still just a job and they're still somebody's employee, just like the rest of corporate America. You can be cut back, demoted, overworked, and many times underpaid. The bottom line: You're not free to choose how you'll spend your time, your greatest asset.

UNIQUELY DESIGNED

Let me pause to clarify here that I'll never, ever be a get-rich-quick proponent who touts instant prosperity through the latest miracle product or financial strategy. I firmly believe each person's financial design should be as individual as their fingerprints. Real estate investment isn't for everyone. Stocks and bonds aren't for everyone. Not everyone is born to be an entrepreneur. But I do believe your financial management style is a reflection of your spiritual life and wellness.

Think about it: Those who approach finances with fear also tend to have a more anxious attitude toward all of life. Those who hold their money with a tightly clenched fist are rarely generous in relationships. Those who take the ostrich approach and bury their heads in the sand when it comes to finances are often not living realistically or authentically in other areas as well. I understand all this because I've worn all those shoes at one point or another.

The design for your personal finances should be as individual as your fingerprints.

I also understand the pain of realizing that you don't have it all under control or have all the answers. For me that pain was most poignant when one of my child's first words turned out to be "bye-bye." Truly, some women are more fulfilled, not to mention sane, in the role of working mom. A great job can give your life purpose and direction. But for me, being separated from my children during the early years was heart-rending.

Leaving them was like undergoing daily surgery; I felt cut off from my true purpose of just being a mom at that time.

FINDING FREEDOM

That's when I genuinely began my study of money. While I appreciated my education and broad book knowledge of business, what I was sold in school wasn't providing me time with my children.

At first my search was confusing, but eventually things got clearer than they'd ever been. What I discovered and applied to my life gave me the power to walk away from my job. It gave me freedom. Certainly when the Bible references freedom, it's usually in a spiritual context. But I believe it also applies to our daily lives in every area, including finances. As I was working up the courage to walk away from a position I'd held for fourteen years, I held on to this verse: "It was for freedom that Christ set us free; therefore keep standing firm and do not be subject again to a yoke of slavery" (Galatians 5:1).

> What does financial freedom truly mean to *you*? What will it look like in *your* situation?

Finally, I walked away from being a wage slave and took hold of financial freedom. Whether you're a struggling young couple (as we were), a single mom, or a woman nearing retirement age without a solid plan for your golden years, you too can grasp freedom through prayer, planning, and action on your part.

What I learned by studying the Proverbs 31 woman changed my life. Throughout history this woman has been modeled and maligned, denounced and praised. Is she too perfect? Or has God given us crucial clues to a financial and life plan that is ageless?

Look again at God's portrait of her in the lines printed below…then join me in the pages that follow as we explore the financial security and freedom we all long for.

A GOD-GIVEN MODEL

An excellent wife, who can find?
For her worth is far above jewels.
The heart of her husband trusts in her,
And he will have no lack of gain.
She does him good and not evil
All the days of her life.
She looks for wool and flax
And works with her hands in delight.
She is like merchant ships;
She brings her food from afar.
She rises also while it is still night
And gives food to her household
And portions to her maidens.
She considers a field and buys it;
From her earnings she plants a vineyard.
She girds herself with strength
And makes her arms strong.
She senses that her gain is good;
Her lamp does not go out at night.
She stretches out her hands to the distaff,
And her hands grasp the spindle.
She extends her hand to the poor,
And she stretches out her hands to the needy.

> "She is sensible that in all her labor there is profit…and this encourages her to go on." (from Matthew Henry's commentary on Proverbs 31)

She is not afraid of the snow for her household,
For all her household are clothed with scarlet.
She makes coverings for herself;
Her clothing is fine linen and purple.
Her husband is known in the gates,
When he sits among the elders of the land.
She makes linen garments and sells them,
And supplies belts to the tradesmen.
Strength and dignity are her clothing,
And she smiles at the future.
She opens her mouth in wisdom,
And the teaching of kindness is on her tongue.
She looks well to the ways of her household,
And does not eat the bread of idleness.
Her children rise up and bless her;
Her husband also, and he praises her, saying:
"Many daughters have done nobly,
But you excel them all."
Charm is deceitful and beauty is vain,
But a woman who fears the LORD, she shall be praised.
Give her the product of her hands,
And let her works praise her in the gates.

(Proverbs 31:10–31)

Part I

CREATE

CHAPTER ONE

The World's First Female Investor

Elizabeth had the perfect life. She had beautiful children and an adoring husband. She was well known and respected in our community. Her husband took care of all the bills and appeared to do so with ease, so she thought she had nothing to worry about when it came to finances.

Until the day her husband passed away.

He left quite a legacy—debts that Elizabeth never knew they had, bills that were unpaid, a welter of financial confusion that took years to decipher and undo. Oh, she did it, and she is much the wiser for what she went through. Elizabeth continues to be a community leader, and she's now a business owner who has done very well. But if only she'd known earlier what *you* will know after reading this book.

FUTURE REALITY

Why, in this new millennium, do many women still think it isn't their responsibility to be good with money? "My husband handles that!" "I'll think about that when I'm older." Knowing and caring about finances is still viewed as a man's job, and talking about money is uncomfortable, to say the least, or garish, to put it more precisely.

And there's still the knight-in-shining-armor syndrome. According to Christopher L. Hayes, author of *Money Makeovers*, one of the myths women still hold on to is that someone's going to rescue them from the burden of financial cares the way knights in shining armor once saved the proverbial damsels in distress.

But here are the facts, according to the National Center for Women and Retirement Research (NCWRR): Of women thirty-five to fifty-five years old, between one-third and two-thirds will be impoverished by age seventy. And women live an average of seven years longer than men. That means many of us will have no choice but to personally handle our own finances at some point. So learn to think about it now!

God never intended you to navigate through life as a slave to money.

I understand your tendency to feel overwhelmed by all this. I've been there. But after reading this book, you'll have the skills, the confidence, and the plan for starting a new financial journey. It's a plan exemplified by a woman whom God placed in the Bible thousands of years ago, yet a plan which can still help you succeed today.

This book is about much more than just managing dollars. It's about finding your purpose in the only One who truly knows what you were created for. That's because God is the One who did the creating. He loved every moment of it and has never stopped loving you. He also never intended for you to navigate your life as a slave to money. Through God, money is subservient to you.

So let's walk down this path together, taking our time and learning to carefully consider our ever-growing number of financial options.

SOMEONE TO LEARN FROM

God can bring a number of people into your life to show you how to be victorious in this very frightening area of life. You can learn from many of them (and from me) in regard to both success and failure.

But as someone to learn from, one person in particular stands out, and I love the fact that she's a woman. I hope you also discover that she's someone much like you, though she lived in an age that was less kind to females than ours, one that didn't afford them all the opportunities we have now. She juggled relationships and career and took it one step further: She became an investor, just as you can. An investor in God. An investor in her family. And an investor in business, in something that would provide financially for her family long into the future. This was her field of dreams, and my goal is to help you consider and find your own field to help provide security for your future and peace in your present.

Let's take a closer look at this remarkable woman from Proverbs 31. Love her or hate her, you have to admit she's a breath of fresh air in a long lineup of other female mug shots depicted in Proverbs. As Ann Spangler and Jean Syswerda observe in *Women of the Bible*, Proverbs overflows with less-than-glowing descriptions of women. There are wayward wives, prostitutes, and women with smoother-than-oil lips. We find strange women, loud women, defiant women, and wives who

are like a continual drip on a rainy day or decay in their husband's bones. There are women whose feet never stay home,
brazen-faced women, and even a woman so repulsive she's
likened to a gold ring in a pig's snout! Yikes!

However, the book of Proverbs opens and closes with positive portrayals of our gender: first, a woman personified as
wisdom (in Proverbs 3–4 and 8–9), then finally, in Proverbs
31, an "excellent wife" who seemingly can do no wrong. In
contrast to the nagging, adulterous, mean-spirited female
images in much of Proverbs, the woman in chapter 31 is God-
fearing, strong, wise, and immensely capable.

> She's God-fearing, strong, wise, and immensely capable.

- She put God at the top of her priority list: "Charm is
  deceitful and beauty is vain, but a woman who fears
  the LORD, she shall be praised" (v. 30).

- She made family her next priority: "She is not afraid
  of the snow for her household, for all her household
  are clothed with scarlet" (v. 21). "Her children rise
  up and bless her" (v. 28).

- She had a positive outlook (for reasons we'll later discuss), and as a result, "she smiles at the future" (v. 25).

- She put her creative talents to work: "She looks for
  wool and flax and works with her hands in delight"
  (v. 13). "She makes linen garments and sells them,
  and supplies belts to the tradesmen" (v. 24).

- She was a careful investor: "She considers a field and
  buys it; from her earnings she plants a vineyard" (v. 16).

- She was a hard worker: "She stretches out her hands to the distaff [a wool-spinning device], and her hands grasp the spindle" (v. 19).

- She was generous: "She extends her hand to the poor, and she stretches out her hands to the needy" (v. 20).

- She was tough: "Strength and dignity are her clothing" (v. 25); she "girds herself with strength and makes her arms strong" (v. 17). And she was tireless: She "rises also while it is still night" (v. 15) and "her lamp does not go out at night" (v. 18).

- She reaped positive rewards: "The heart of her husband trusts in her, and he will have no lack of gain" (v. 11). "Give her the product of her hands, and let her works praise her in the gates" (v. 31).

Do you hate her yet? Many women do because her example has been thrown into the faces of ordinary women who feel they can't possibly live up to her standards.

But let's take another look.

PROVEN

Did this woman truly exist, with all these positive attributes? Or was she simply a figment of the author's wishful imagination in creating a model for the rest of us to follow?

I don't think it matters. If we believe all Scripture is God-inspired and beneficial for our training in righteousness, then

Determine to apply a proven, winning plan to your personal finances.

we must also accept that there are many lessons to be learned from the woman in Proverbs 31—lessons of family, virtue, and honor. And in this book, I'll focus especially on the financial lessons she teaches us.

I've decided to give this capable lady a fictional name, because referring to her as only "the Proverbs 31 woman" can seem so distant and impersonal. So I've named her "Proven"—combining the beginning of the word *Proverbs* and the last letters of *women*.

Proverbs + women = a Proven, winning plan

Clearly, Proven was very much involved in her family's financial life. She made linen garments and sold them. She considered a field and bought it; from her earnings she planted a vineyard. And remember, this resourceful lady didn't have a laptop or any other high-tech tools to work with. Proven worked with what she had at the time.

Notice that the passage doesn't say her husband did all the work and gave her a shopping allowance. In fact, it mentions that she plants a vineyard with her own earnings. She created both immediate and future wealth and provision for her family.

Proven's model for financial well-being can be summed up in three simple words: *create, consider*, and *invest*. She created products, she considered her field of investment, and then she actually bought it!

You can do the same thing in your life—in God's unique way for you.

OUR INVESTMENT RESPONSIBILITY

Proven's model for the role we should play in our family's finances is consistent with New Testament lessons on money. The Gospel of Matthew records a story Jesus told to illustrate our financial responsibilities. It begins with a man who went on a trip and left his servants money (also referred to as "talents") to invest—each according to his ability. He gave one servant five talents, another two talents, and the last servant one talent.

Away he went, and the servants went to work—or at least two of them did—taking risks, doubling their money, and receiving a reward and praise from their boss when he got back home. But the last servant was afraid and buried his talent in the sand. Sound familiar? It does to me.

Let's read about this last guy as the moment came to face his boss:

"For I can do everything with the help of Christ who gives me the strength I need."
(Philippians 4:13 NLT)

"He said, 'Sir, I know that you are a hard man. You gather grain where you have not planted. You take up where you have not spread out. I was afraid and I hid your money in the ground. See! Here is your money.'

"His owner said to him, 'You bad and lazy servant. You knew that I gather grain where I have not planted. You knew that I take up where I have not spread out. You should have taken my money to the bank. When I came back, I could have had my own money and what the bank paid for using it. Take the one piece of money from him. Give it to the one who has ten pieces of money.'

"For the man who has will have more given to him.
He will have more than enough. The man who has
nothing, even what he has will be taken away." (Matthew
25:24–29, NLV)

Talk about harsh! Harsh *reality*, that is. God watches and
hopes we'll multiply our money! But how many of us are more
like the last slave, who buried the piece of silver in the ground?
Certainly, one perspective is that he was lazy and indifferent.
But I think this poor fellow was simply afraid, and to that I can
certainly relate.

At times in my life I not only buried my head in the sand,
but also essentially flushed my money down the toilet. I was
more incompetent than the last servant because I spent everything I made as soon as I got it, and more. It took a long time
for me to realize it was my responsibility not only to make
money but to multiply it.

As a young woman, I didn't give this too much consideration until my children were born. God, however, has always
taken it very seriously.

So exactly how do you double your money in today's
tumultuous economy? You have more options than you know,
and we'll discuss many of them as we learn to create, consider,
and invest like the good servants and the Proverbs 31 woman.

By putting Proven's money model into action in my life, I
was able to give careful consideration to my days and how I
spent them. As we'll see, whoever or whatever Proven is, she's at
the very least an attainable and realistic example for today's
women who long to be free and to have meaningful, prosper-

ous lives. Yes, it's true. But it's not easy. I must tell you that this book will require action on your part. It will require you to examine your life and create a new plan.

Is the Proverbs 31 model attainable on your own? Not a chance. Can you do all things through Christ who strengthens you (Philippians 4:13)? Absolutely! So say a prayer, get ready to face your fears, and extract your head and talents from the sand. Get ready to transform your financial life based on a plan that has been "proven" time and again.

CHAPTER TWO

God's Vision for Your Success

When have you been most prosperous in your life? When have you felt God's power working in and through you? I believe our Proverbs 31 woman was working in the zone—the synergy of endeavor and result in which life seems to run more smoothly, where everything seems to fall effortlessly into place. Don't laugh. I've been a lifelong dieter, and my favorite health guru is Dr. Barry Sears of *The Zone* fame. He describes the zone as a place where your mind is relaxed yet alert and exquisitely focused. Meanwhile the body is fluid, strong, and apparently indefatigable. You feel almost euphoric. Athletes describe the zone as the place where they can run without tiring or where a basketball player sees the hoop as twice its size, never missing a shot.

There are various theories as to why the zone phenomenon happens physically, mentally, and spiritually. Based on results in my life, I get in the zone simply when I'm smack-dab in the middle of God's will for my life. When I step outside His will,

I step outside the zone. Life gets tough, and twice as much effort is expended for half of the results.

Much of this has to do with where my priorities are at the time. My real priorities. Just as your car needs a tune-up, you may need a tune-in—a moment to step back and evaluate what's really important to you and where you've been—before you can honestly move forward.

MEETING WITH YOUR CEO

That's why meeting with our CEO is so important. No, not the guy who signs your paychecks. I'm talking about your real boss—God. When we bring all this before Him in an open and humble way and ask Him to examine our priorities and help us make any needed adjustments, He always shows up.

Here's a prayer we could all use:

Do you have a clear vision for your life and the life of your family?

Search me, O God, and know my heart; try me and know my anxious thoughts; and see if there be any hurtful way in me, and lead me in the everlasting way. (Psalm 139:23–24)

Another version puts it this way:

God, see what is in my heart. Know what is there. Put me to the test. Know what I'm thinking. See if there's anything in my life you don't like. Help me live in the way that is always right. (NIrV)

Proven must have prayed something like that. Based on her actions, she seems to have had a clear vision—God's vision— for her life and the life of her family. It may appear she didn't struggle at all with questions about what that vision was, but come on, she was human too! She must have struggled at one point or another. We all question what exactly it is we're doing here. And if we simply take that question to God, He'll give us the answer. Instead of thinking, "What's my plan for my life?" ask God, "What is *Your* plan for my life?"

But here's the problem: Unless we're spending time with Him, how can we hear His voice?

One day when I was having a time of prayer and reading, I began daydreaming and eventually fell asleep. So much for showing respect to the person I was meeting with, right? As I awakened with a start, I realized I would never behave this way if I were meeting with my boss at my workplace. Can you imagine sitting in the big guy's office for your annual evaluation, when you suddenly begin staring at the walls before falling into a deep slumber? You would be fired! But that's how I was treating my time with the real Big Guy. Yes, God is merciful and understanding even when we fall asleep. Remember Peter and the disciples who couldn't keep watch with Jesus for an hour? But if we're seeking direction and guidance from the true Chief Executive Officer, perhaps we should approach Him as such.

Many people like to call this a "devotional time" or a "quiet time." I call this my meeting with my CEO. Knowing that "I can do all things through Christ who strengthens me" (Philippians 4:13, NKJV), I know conversely that I can do nothing without Him. Really! Or at least nothing very well.

Many times in my life, God has astonishingly used this meeting with Him as a precise guide to get me through the trials of the day. Without this time with God, I invariably flounder. If I take just a few moments to quiet my mind and my heart, my entire day goes by more smoothly, and I feel more capable in managing challenges.

In Jeremiah 29:11, the Lord promises His people that He has a plan for us, to give us a future and a hope. What He says next is this:

> "Then you will call upon Me and come and pray to Me, and I will listen to you. You will seek Me and find Me when you search for Me with all your heart. I will be found by you," declares the LORD. (Jeremiah 29:12–14)

God will be found by you if you seek Him and search for Him with all your heart.

Have you ever been discouraged when it seems God isn't listening or maybe He's forgotten about you? I have. And though He hasn't forgotten us or stopped listening, we have to persevere. Keep searching and keep meeting with your Chief Executive Officer, and He and His plans will become clear.

Knowing God's vision in this way makes all the difference in whether we succeed in getting a handle on our financial life. And that, my friend, takes time—plus patient, believing prayer:

> If any of you lacks wisdom, let him ask of God, who gives to all generously and without reproach, and it will be given to him. But he must ask in faith without any

doubting, for the one who doubts is like the surf of the sea, driven and tossed by the wind. (James 1:5–6)

We've all been confused. I know what it's like to feel full of doubt and tossed by the wind. As a young woman, this seemed to be my perpetual state. But as I've grown older and hopefully a bit wiser, I know without any doubt that God answers us when we call to Him. It may not be instantaneous, and it may not be the answer you're looking for, but He gives us the right answer that's best for us and our situation.

When we ask for wisdom, God always, always delivers. That's a promise. And after you've asked for help, expect answers. Expect action on the Lord's part and learn to wait for Him.

> "I know the plans I have for you," announces the Lord. "I want you to enjoy success. I do not plan to harm you. I will give you hope for the years to come." (Jeremiah 29:11 NIrV)

YOUR UNIQUE PURPOSE

In deciding to walk away from my "safe" job and consider other options, nothing felt right, and I was completely confused as to which direction my life should go. It was one of many times in my life when I felt thoroughly lost and exhausted.

One pivotal morning, not only did I get on my knees, I lay flat on the ground and prayed, "Lord, what is it that *You* would have me do with this life? Instead of always asking You to get on board with my plans, what is it that You require of me? Today I lay my life and all my plans before You and not only ask for Your guidance, I ask You to take this life and make it Yours."

Later that day I got a call from a producer at the Christian Broadcasting Network to tell me about an open position doing something I'd only dreamed of: working for a talk and information program for women, reaching out to them for Jesus. How's that for an answer to prayer? That day!

This was further proof that God has a unique purpose for each of us. He has a vision that's uniquely suited to our talents, personality, and temperament.

He has *always* had this vision for you. "For we are God's workmanship, created in Christ Jesus to do good works, which God prepared in advance for us to do" (Ephesians 2:10, NIV). Did you catch that? Prepared in advance! He could barely wait until you were born so He could bless you by fulfilling this purpose in you. God determined beforehand that those who believe in Christ will be adopted into His family and conformed to His Son:

> He chose us in Him before the foundation of the world, that we would be holy and blameless before Him. In love He predestined us to adoption as sons through Jesus Christ to Himself, according to the kind intention of His will, to the praise of the glory of His grace, which He freely bestowed on us in the Beloved. (Ephesians 1:4–6)

He has a unique purpose for your life that flows out of His love. Your job is to seek that vision and then follow His lead.

Action Application

At this point, I'm asking you to move from passive reader to active participant—to be a doer of the Word, not just a hearer.

His unique purpose for your life flows out of His love for you.

God loves action, so this is where we begin applying these principles to our financial lives.

Take out your schedule book and set a meeting time with God, your real CEO. He'll help direct you through times of prosperity and times of challenge. Put this meeting on your daily planner and treat it as if you're meeting with your boss at work. Isn't this Boss much more important?

As you plan to seek God's direction, here are a few questions to think about:

- When in your life have you felt God's leading? Write down one time when you've sensed God's direction in your life and you followed it.

- How did things turn out for you?

- How did you feel during the process—frightened or elated?

- Now remember a time when you sensed God's direction and turned away from it. What happened then?

"You shall remember the LORD your God, for it is He who is giving you power to make wealth, that He may confirm His covenant which He swore to your fathers, as it is this day." (Deuteronomy 8:18)

ASSESS YOUR INTERESTS AND TALENTS

The Proverbs 31 money model begins with the ability to *create* by working with your hands and your mind.

Traditionally, Hebrew women spent huge amounts of time spinning and weaving material for clothing, rugs, and other household needs. These were resourceful women who took wool from sheep or fibers from plants like cotton and flax and spun them into thread. Some linen was so finely woven that it formed silky, rich material. Waterproof tents and coats were made with heavy cloth from goat or camel hair.

These women were hard-working and amazingly creative. Proven adds another element: She was energetic, working in delight. When she wasn't sewing clothes, making belts, or negotiating with tradesmen, she was looking for wool and flax and bringing her wares from all over the city to be sold at market. She made clothes for herself and her family using the finest material she could find.

I get tired just thinking about her life. But you have to admit she was creative—and so are *you*. God made each of us to creatively use the resources He provides. You may believe you'll never live up to Proven's ideals and standards. Maybe none of us will. But I believe it was God's intention to provide through this woman a model for financial responsibility and success. How you recreate that model in your own life is completely up to you.

Unlike the Proverbs 31 woman, I'll never work with wool or flax, and my hands will never grasp the spindle. I have no idea how to make a linen garment or a belt, and I can't imagine what my clothes or my children's clothes would look like if I ever tried to make them myself. This isn't where my interest lies, and it never will be, unless God changes me into a different person. I can, however, work with words and video to create compelling and life-changing stories. Speaking on Christ's behalf, I can use the mediums of television and radio to tell people about Him.

To help you create in a way that's all your own, God will use what you're naturally drawn to. Do you like to create with your hands, as Proven did? Do you like to create with your mind? She had that covered as well, in the way she considered her investment options. In all of creation, there's no one exactly like you. God made you unique and special. Extraordinary! Do you feel that way? You should. You are His creation and He adores you. Now, what will you do with all the talents and creative intelligence He has given to you?

You are creative. God made each of us to creatively use the resources He provides.

Some people question whether we're born with talents or they're simply learned. If talents are learned, Michael Jordan was the most astute student to ever set foot on a basketball court, and Julie Andrews must have had some killer voice lessons. The obvious truth is that we're all born with special gifts, and if we take time to quiet our minds, to pray, and to listen to God's still, small voice, we'll know in our hearts where our true talents are.

If the foot says, "Because I am not a hand, I am not a part of the body," it is not for this reason any the less a part of the body. And if the ear says, "Because I am not an eye, I am not a part of the body," it is not for this reason any the less a part of the body. If the whole body were an eye, where would the hearing be? If the whole were hearing, where would the sense of smell be? But now God has placed the members, each one of them, in

the body, just as He desired. If they were all one member, where would the body be? But now there are many
members, but one body. (1 Corinthians 12:15–20)

God has appointed gifts in the church (1 Corinthians
12:4–20), and God has also given you gifts and talents to use
in your family life, community life, and business.

You can take a number of tests to determine and assess the
gifts or talents possessed by you or someone in your family.
Fine. Take those tests, but take them with a grain of salt. The
Holy Spirit's direction is a better guide to assess your true
talents. And He may surprise you. He may astound you with a
talent that no test designer has ever thought of.

But here's the tough part in determining your true gifts:
Sometimes they differ from your interests. For example, you
may love to listen to music, but if you don't have the singing
voice to support that interest, don't even think about quitting
your day job to be a full-time vocalist. You may love to watch
baseball on television, but becoming a major league pitcher is
just a major dream.

But take heart. God has a special calling for your life. Can
you sense this mission? Or is it so far buried under anxiety and
day-to-day responsibilities that you've forgotten who you are in
Him? You may be overwhelmed with just getting by, working in
a job that saps the spirit right out of you just to put food on the
table. That kind of joyless existence isn't God's will for your life.
He loves you. He created you for a special purpose. You're a wonderful creation, made complete in the image of God for His
glory. For a moment, think about God's creation—the expansive

Through intellect,
will, and emotion—
you are "a show-
case for God's
glorious character."

universe, the miracle of a tiny atom, the beautiful and bountiful earth. But in all of God's creation, nothing compares with you.

In *Search for Significance*, Robert S. McGee explains that when God first created human beings, our God-given purpose was to reflect His glory:

> Through man, God wanted to demonstrate His holiness (Ps. 99:3–5); love and patience (1 Cor. 13:4); forbearance (1 Cor. 13:7); wisdom (James 3:13, 17); comfort (2 Cor. 1:3–4); forgiveness (Heb. 10:17); faithfulness (Ps. 89:1–2, 5, 8); and grace (Ps. 111:4). Through his intellect, free will, and emotions, man was to be the showcase for God's glorious character.[1]

That was God's desire and His creative expression of it. That's *you*—a showcase for God's glorious character! Get back to your heart's desire and *His* heart's desire, and when they're one and the same, that's when life works. In fact, that's when life rocks! That's when living is wonderful, beyond every expectation. So never limit yourself or your children. You are God's creation.

Action Application

Assess your own creative interests and make a list:

- What do you love doing? What have you always loved doing?

- What are you naturally drawn to?

- What makes you feel the most creative?

Now find a quiet place and ask God this question: "What are my true talents and how can I use them for You?" Over the next few days, write down His answers, and thank Him for them, as David did:

> I will give thanks to You, for I am fearfully and wonderfully made; wonderful are Your works, and my soul knows it very well. (Psalm 139:14)

YOUR MISSION STATEMENT

Now you're ready to put His vision for your success into a simple statement. Most successful companies are directed and focused by a mission statement or a statement of purpose. For example, at IBM, it's this: "Our goal is simply stated. We want to be the best service organization in the world." And at Wal-Mart: "To give ordinary folks the chance to buy the same things as rich people." One of Nike's mission statements was simply, "Crush Reebok."

Have you ever sat down and established your own mission statement, your statement of purpose for your years on this earth? Not until I was in my late thirties did I actually put the statement on paper. I like simplicity, so mine states: "To love God, serve Him, and speak His name at every opportunity." From that purpose, all subsequent goals concerning family, work, and community are directed. Proverbs 4:26 tells us, "Watch the path of your feet and all your ways will be established." Or as another version expresses it, "Know where you are headed, and you will stay on solid ground" (CEV).

So many times in life we're running and running, but we have no idea where we're going. Where's the finish line to this rat race? While working in traditional news reporting, most of the time I could relate to those rats. And I'm not talking about the personality of reporters! (We're not all that bad, I promise.) As a "rat" I worked hard and ran fast on my wheel, but I never got anywhere. At the end of the day I was in the same place where I'd started. Thankfully, the Lord helped me see this futile race I was in before it was too late. It gave me time to plan a jump for freedom.

"I cry out to God Most High…and he carries out his plan for me."
(Psalm 57:2 NIrV)

Action Application

Write out your mission statement, using your own words and following your own heart. Your mission statement should be focused but flexible. It should also be concise, realistic, and achievable. It need not sound religious, nor does it have to be patterned after the mission of some Fortune 500 company. But it does have to reflect *you*.

In my statement I included the phrase "speak His name" because it's the one thing I know I can do. I can talk (and talk, and talk, my husband would probably say). Why not use this strength/weakness for good and for God?

After you've written your own mission statement, don't show it to anyone else until you've had time to think and pray about it for a while.

Let me remind you once more: God has a purpose for you. How does your mission statement reflect that purpose?

"For I know the plans that I have for you," declares the LORD, "plans for welfare and not for calamity to give you a future and a hope." (Jeremiah 29:11)

FACE FEARS

When you read Proverbs 31, does this woman seem like someone who lives her life paralyzed by fear? No, quite the opposite. We may never attain all the character traits of this beautiful and capable woman, but we can learn from her. When Proven faced fear, she tackled it head-on. It had to be frightening for a woman in her day to "consider a field and buy it" (v. 16). It had to be overwhelming taking care of her family, creating products for the tradesmen, and all while planting a vineyard. Talk about fear of failure! In that society, men would quickly laugh at her should she make a mistake. And yet we read that she "smiles at the future" (v. 25).

Another version expresses that verse this way: "She can laugh at the days that are coming" (v. 25, NIrV). And so can *you*. You can laugh at the days that are coming, because if you're trusting in the Lord, your success is guaranteed according to God's plan. Does that mean things will always be easy or turn out the way you'd hoped and planned? Of course not. God uses times of hardship and trial to shape our character. Yes, you'll experience tough times and challenges, but you will prevail. That's a promise from Him. No one who puts their trust in Him will ever be forsaken. Listen to what He tells His people:

"Do not fear, for I am with you; do not anxiously look about you, for I am your God. I will strengthen you,

Trusting in the Lord, you can laugh at the days that are coming.

surely I will help you, surely I will uphold you with My
righteous right hand." (Isaiah 41:10)

I once interviewed Nicky Marone, author of *How to Mother
a Successful Daughter*. In this book she notes how many girls are
bold and adventurous before the age of twelve, not really caring
what the boys think but still curious about their environment
and enthusiastic about exploring and trying new things. When
they reach age twelve, something changes. Their self-esteem
takes a dive; many lower their aspirations, while self-doubt takes
over. I believe this is the age when children need parents the
most. Yes, every day and moment of every year are important in
a child's life, each one potentially life-changing and life-affirming.
I've witnessed this in raising two daughters and a stepson. But
during the early teenage years, our children come face-to-face with
fear, and they'll learn either to handle it or to succumb to it. The
choice they make will impact their lives forever.

So if you're a parent, step in and encourage your children,
especially your teenage girls, to look fear boldly in the face and
to "laugh at the days to come." Remind them that perfect love
(God's love) can cast out fear (1 John 4:18). Teach them to say
with David, "When I am afraid, I will put my confidence in
you" (Psalm 56:3, TLB).

Besides, there's no easier strategy for overcoming a fear than
simply to face it and deal with it. During one of my meetings with
my CEO, I read a KLOVE radio network devotional for inspira-
tion. In a few paragraphs on overcoming fear, there was a story
about Alice, a homemaker who'd been married for thirty years to
Richard, a businessman who had always taken care of their family's

money matters. Alice's biggest fear was that she'd be left alone.

To overcome a fear, the easiest strategy is this: Simply face it and deal with it.

She'd often tell her friends she hoped she would pass away before Richard because she didn't feel she could handle life by herself.

But when Richard had a stroke, Alice was placed in the position of having to care for him plus make all the financial decisions for them both. At first it was frightening, overwhelming, and nerve-wracking. But once she began to take responsibility, she made a life-changing discovery: Security doesn't lie in having things, but in handling them. She found that facing her fears was simple compared to the years she'd wasted feeling inadequate, helpless, and dependent.

You're not the only person to have fears about finances. Face your fears, and you'll overcome them.

Action Application

Take a piece of paper and list your greatest fears about money. Be honest with God on this because He knows how you feel anyway.

Now put a check mark beside each fear you listed that's too great for God to handle—you know, the things that might scare Him.

What, no checks? Good! Now rip up this paper and learn the lesson from Alice: Facing your fears is much more empowering than running from them.

> There is no fear in love; but perfect love casts out fear, because fear involves punishment, and the one who fears is not perfected in love. (1 John 4:18)

FACE FAILURE

"Yes, you will fail. You'll take some hits. But keep going; don't shut the door on opportunity."

Those words were some of the best advice I received from a financial adviser named Doreen Roadman, from Virginia Beach, who has been the expert in some of my financial stories over the years. It echoes the same advice from another one of my favorites, Robert Kiyosaki of *Rich Dad, Poor Dad* fame, whom I met and interviewed while attending his investing seminar in Phoenix. What I've learned from these wise individuals has set me free—free to fail, that is.

Here's the harsh reality: You will fail. You absolutely will be disappointed in life. You'll make some bad decisions. Welcome to the world. So instead of avoiding failure, learn from it.

In another book, *Cashflow Quadrant*, Kiyosaki tells us to expect to be disappointed: "Just as inside every problem lies an opportunity, inside every disappointment lies a priceless gem of wisdom."[2] Accepting failure requires something that can be equally difficult—humility. We won't succeed all the time. But remember, "God is opposed to the proud, but gives grace to the humble" (James 4:6).

Be free to fail… because at times you will fail.

When you fell down as a toddler, did your mother tell you to stop walking altogether so you could avoid such tumbles in the future? When you skinned your knee, did she tell you to give up playing on the playground so you wouldn't encounter such disappointments? Of course not! She encouraged you to get up and try again.

Permit me to momentarily step into the role of your

own mother: When you fall, get up and try again!

Do you remember what you learned in school about someone who was unsuccessful as a young man in a retail business, lost a number of elections for public office, and suffered from attacks of depression? Yet he became one of the greatest men in American history: President Abraham Lincoln.

Yes, you'll fail. Guess what? So will everyone else. The question is this: *When* you do fail, will you drop out of the game, or will you learn from your experience?

My guess is that Proven didn't consider just one field before she made her purchase. The fact that she *considered* at all means she did some comparison shopping. She had to look at some disappointing sites before settling on the investment that would feed her family by providing a source of income. Do you think all her belts and linen garments were always perfect? She had to learn, and she probably had to fail before she reached the point where her works praised her in the gates.

Face and even embrace failure. Learning its lessons can propel you to the greatest success in your life.

We all have our challenges and our weaknesses, just like Proven. While it's important to acknowledge what we can do well and what we can't, we must also acknowledge that God is greater than all of it. You might say, "I'm not good with math, I could never be an investor." Math wasn't my favorite either. But instead of running from financial responsibility, take this challenge to God, the Great Mathematician, who will help us understand the numbers in spite of ourselves.

We might say, "I simply don't understand investing." That

may truly be the case now, but try taking that weakness before God, the source of all knowledge. Ask Him for wisdom, and He will deliver.

The apostle Paul wrote,

> I say to everyone among you not to think more highly of himself than he ought to think; but to think so as to have sound judgment, as God has allotted to each a measure of faith. (Romans 12:3)

Paul was speaking here particularly of our spiritual gifts in relation to the church, but I believe this is also a practical verse that should be applied to all of our lives. Not that we should put ourselves down, but we should view ourselves objectively, with sound judgment and sober-mindedness, so as not to think too highly of ourselves. That means admitting and facing our weaknesses and failures. Not easy, is it? But our weaknesses should never be used as excuses to avoid taking action. In fact, when we're weak, He is strong.

Do you recall the story of Moses confronting Pharaoh and leading the Hebrews out of Egypt? And yet Moses had a speech impediment. Imagine him being sent to speak to Egypt's all-powerful ruler on behalf of the Hebrews when he had problems speaking clearly to anyone about anything. Yes, Moses had his brother Aaron to help him, but he was still the guy in charge and had to rely on God for every move. When he was weak, God was strong.

Another case in point: Consider the apostle Paul and his "thorn in the flesh" (2 Corinthians 12:7). Paul writes,

Concerning this I implored the Lord three times that it might leave me. And He has said to me, "My grace is sufficient for you, for power is perfected in weakness." Most gladly, therefore, I will rather boast about my weaknesses, so that the power of Christ may dwell in me. Therefore I am well content with weaknesses, with insults, with distresses, with persecutions, with difficulties, for Christ's sake; for when I am weak, then I am strong. (2 Corinthians 12:8–10)

Embrace your failure, and learn its lessons.

Action Application

Take your failures and weaknesses before God, as Paul did. Be honest and write down what you've been avoiding because of your perceived weakness.

What step can you take today to move from excuse to action?

Pray—and watch His strength become perfected in you, as you rely on the Holy Spirit's help:

The Spirit…helps our weakness; for we do not know how to pray as we should, but the Spirit Himself intercedes for us with groanings too deep for words; and He who searches the hearts knows what the mind of the Spirit is, because He intercedes for the saints according to the will of God. (Romans 8:26–27)

NO BLAME, ALL GAIN

There seems to be an element conspicuously missing from the Proverbs 31 story—her husband's role in her business plan. He's seen giving a positive reaction to her, he's known to sit among the elders of the land, but nowhere is he seen considering a field with his wife and making the real estate purchase or creating products and selling them for an income. It is Proven herself who considers a field and buys it. *She* plants a vineyard. *She* does all the work that we see accomplished here.

I think this passage is written this way intentionally, as all things are when inspired by God. Though it's reasonable to assume that the husband wasn't excluded from all of Proven's financial endeavors, I believe this passage is written this way so that all women ever since have a role model of someone who takes responsibility for herself and her family in every way, including financially.

> Focus on *your* responsibility—a better path than blaming others.

We don't see Proven blaming her husband for being lazy, or nagging him to get a better, higher-paying job. This was a woman of action. Instead of focusing on what her mate was or wasn't doing, she was focusing on her own work—at home, in the community, and in her business. Let's be honest: What wife hasn't tried to change her spouse by some subtle suggestion for improvement or not-so-subtle criticism that deflates his precarious ego? It doesn't work, does it? Proven teaches us a better path—to love God, take care of our families and community, and take care of our finances, while enjoying the rewards of our hard work. She teaches us to take responsibility and to blame no one.

STRENGTHEN YOURSELF

To successfully manage our families and our finances, we must take care of ourselves! Why is it we still feel guilty about that? I don't know about you, but I still get a pang of guilt taking an hour away from my family to go to an exercise class.

It's time for all of us to get over that, just as Proven did: "She girds herself with strength and makes her arms strong" (v. 17). This lady stayed in shape physically, mentally, and spiritually. She had to! And so do you.

I'll never forget a story I heard about a young woman who stopped her car at a gas station. As she got out to fill her car's tank, a poor, bedraggled teenager drove up at the pump beside her and said, "I seem to be out of money. Would you mind filling my gas tank for me?" Taking pity on the poor teen, she replied, "Sure, I'll help you out." After the woman filled the car, the teenager thanked her and drove away.

"On the day I called, You answered me; You made me bold with strength in my soul." (Psalm 138:3)

Meanwhile, a lady had driven up at the next pump. "You seem to be so nice," the lady said, after observing the woman's help for the teenager. "I've forgotten my purse at home; would you mind filling my gas tank for me?"

Wanting to live up to her "nice" reputation, the young woman once again smiled and complied.

Then a man who had driven up began talking to the young woman, marveling at how generous she was. He too asked for a free tank of gas. Basking in the glow of his praise, the young woman again filled another person's tank.

When she was finally free to take care of her own car, she reached deep into her pocketbook, but she now had no money to fill her own gas tank. She was no longer able to help either herself or anyone else.

"How ridiculous," you say. "Who would ever do something like that?" We do, every day! Giving is fine as long as you aren't neglecting your own gas tank. But are you giving away too much of your time and energy and feeling resentful because of it? You cannot adequately care for your family, run a business, and give back to the community unless you take time to strengthen your own body and mind and heart. Even Jesus retreated from the crowds for times to pray. Don't let yourself run on empty, or you'll be unable to help anyone.

Action Application

As a woman, you most likely know how it feels to give and give until you're absolutely spent. There's just nothing left.

Consider taking time alone to think through these questions:

- Today, how can you fill your own gas tank?

- Where and when are you running on empty?

- Who are you blaming for your financial problems? Are you ready to accept full responsibility for what you do and do not have?

- Now, what can you do today to make a positive difference in your family's financial future?

As you take this time alone, remember that even Jesus took time to recharge, even when His life was at its busiest:

The news about him spread all the more, so that crowds of people came to hear him and to be healed of their sicknesses. But Jesus often withdrew to lonely places and prayed. (Luke 5:15–16, NIV)

TAKE A STEP

For many years I hosted a kids' talk show in Virginia, and I had the opportunity to speak to lots of students both in and away from the studio. On the subject of deciding what they wanted to do with their lives, I always counseled them to do the thing that scared them. Don't settle. Do the thing you've always wanted to do but were afraid to because it seemed too big for you.

It requires you first to take a step in that direction. Just one step.

Can you imagine how Moses felt when he encountered a talking, burning bush telling him to go free God's people in Egypt? Moses responded as most of us would—with doubt and incredulity.

But Moses said, "They won't believe me! They won't do what I tell them to. They'll say, 'Jehovah never appeared to you!'"

"What do you have there in your hand?" The Lord asked him.

And he replied, "A shepherd's rod."

"Throw it down on the ground," the Lord told him. So he threw it down—and it became a serpent, and Moses ran from it!

Then the Lord told him, "Grab it by the tail!" He did, and it became a rod in his hand again! (Exodus 4:1–4, TLB)

Your very first step will be the scariest...and then it gets easier.

Okay, stop here. Sure, Moses continued on with his self-doubt, saying he wasn't a strong speaker. Sure, God was getting a bit impatient with Moses. But give the guy some credit! He grabbed the serpent by the tail! Moses could have kept running. He didn't have to turn back, reach down his hand, and obey. I'm terrified by the thought of grabbing a serpent by the tail, especially if a burning bush was telling me to do so. But Moses took that step. Then another step. And another. Before he knew it he was crossing the Red Sea in one of the most amazing miracles ever.

Your very first step will be the scariest, but then it begins to get easier. And once you take that first step, God will entrust you with more and more. I'll never forget taking the first step to become a real estate investor. Okay, I know it's no burning-bush snake-handling experience, but for me it was terrifying. I trembled while signing the first contract. In the car I prayed, "O Lord, what have I just done?" He replied, "Something." I'd just done *something*—something that would eventually help buy my freedom from being a wage slave. It was the first step and it was the hardest, but it qualified and prepared me for more. As Jesus said,

"Suppose you can be trusted with very little. Then you can be trusted with a lot. But suppose you are not honest with very little. Then you will not be honest with a lot. Suppose you have not been worthy of trust in handling

worldly wealth. Then who will trust you with true riches?
Suppose you have not been worthy of trust in handling
someone else's property. Then who will give you property
of your own? No servant can serve two masters at the
same time. He will hate one of them and love the other.
Or he will be faithful to one and dislike the other. You
can't serve God and Money at the same time." (Luke
16:10–13, NIrV)

Serve God, not money, and you will prosper. God wants to
know He can trust you with true riches, spiritual riches, so now
is the time to take the first step. Start small to create something
you love.

I've mentioned how I truly believe each person's investment
style is as individual as their fingerprint. No one can give you a
set plan or road map on how to create, consider, and invest,
because God has a unique plan for you and your finances. It
includes the "wool" and "flax" you'll find to create your products, which in your case may be a computer and phone
allowing you to begin a home-based business. It includes the
field you'll consider and purchase. In your case, that may mean
developing and patenting a fabulous idea you've always had in
the back of your mind.

We're learning from Proven to first create, consider, and
invest. Now develop your own style in doing so. Innovate, invent,
originate, and dream—as you did when you were a child.

Consider Lillian Vernon, the founder and CEO of the
Lillian Vernon Corporation, a catalog company specializing in
household and children's products. In her youth in the 1930s,

Lillian's family fled the Nazis in Germany and eventually settled in the United States. After World War II, as a young wife pregnant with her first child, she used savings from wedding gift money to buy a $495 advertisement in *Seventeen* magazine for personalized purses and belts. She received $32,000 in orders from that ad—and her mail-order business was launched.

Today her company has revenues of $287 million and 5,300 employees. She worked with her hands, at her kitchen table, I might add, to create a product that would launch her biggest investment—her business. Nobody could have planned that track for her. She had to find it herself, just as you will as you fully rely on God's help and direction.

Consider for a moment how creative God was in making you—His investment. There's no one exactly like you anywhere on this earth. Never has been. You're unique, extraordinary, and matchless in His eyes.

David understood this well, and he acknowledged it to God:

You formed my inward parts; You wove me in my mother's womb. I will give thanks to You, for I am fearfully and wonderfully made; wonderful are Your works, and my soul knows it very well. (Psalm 139:13–14)

God *loved* creating you! He enjoyed being the first Artist and Architect. What kind of mind could possibly create and form such wonderful and complex animals, plants, and human beings! I get the feeling He savored every moment of those first six days played out in Genesis.

Then God looked over all he had made, and he saw that it was excellent in every way. (Genesis 1:31, NLT)

Create something...so that when it's finished, you can say, "Now that's good!"

When was the last time you created something, large or small, and when it was finished you said, "Now, that's *good!*" When was the last time you poured passion into your work, crafting and caring about every detail? When was the last time you were completely spent because of the energy you expended in bringing something new into this world?

Action Application

Create something you love. But this item isn't for sale; this is for *you*. Make it something you've always wanted to do. Something that scares you a bit! Something about which you've often said, "*Someday* I'll do that."

Someday is here! Savor it.

Don't tell anyone about this project; it's just between you and God.

Part II

CONSIDER

CHAPTER THREE

Before You Buy the Field

Look again at Proverbs 31:16, where we read that Proven "considers a field and buys it; from her earnings she plants a vineyard." Nearly every English translation uses the word *consider* here. Dictionaries tell us that *to consider* means to fix your mind on something in order to understand it. It means to reflect on something with care, to ponder it, to study it, to meditate on it. It means to attentively and carefully view or observe or examine something, to think about it seriously, maturely, or carefully.

Seriously…maturely…carefully. That's the sum total of how we should handle every investment. We should approach opportunities with much thought and observation in order to fully understand them.

THINK WITH CARE

Consideration is the opposite approach to the one taken by the wicked, lazy slave in the Parable of the Talents (money) discussed in Matthew 25. The servant who received only one talent went away and buried this money in the ground. Not too much consideration there. The other slaves traded their talents and were able to double their money—which is no small return in the investment world! That type of yield takes thought, reflection, and finally action.

In *Beautiful in God's Eyes*, Elizabeth George describes our Proverbs 31 woman as a lady of "triple action" including consideration, acquisition, and renovation.[3] Putting on her businesswoman hat, she carefully looks at the field to determine whether it would be a wise investment. In her heart she wants a field, but choosing instead to let her mind take control, she sets out to learn all she can about that piece of property.

Now stop here! Have you ever gone house hunting? Even if you're not yet a homeowner, you've certainly been like me on a Sunday afternoon, driving by houses and dreaming of the future. I love to look at houses and properties, and if I'm honest, I know this is because it's completely tied to my emotions. I fall in love with houses, because to me it means the fulfillment of a dream. Who doesn't tie property to dreams of a family in a warm and safe home, with children playing in the backyard?

Consideration takes *time*—time to think.

Although dreams are exciting, another lesson I learned from Proven when I became a real estate investor was to put my emotions on hold when looking at a property and, after much prayer, to let my mind make the decision, as opposed to my feelings. Making sound, rational decisions is a "proven" strategy.

Elizabeth George goes on to describe how the Proverbs 31 woman might have put consideration into action. First, she would find out the value of the property by collecting solid information, not relying on hearsay or even on "expert" opinion alone. She would also examine the property herself. I know many real estate investors who have bought a property sight unseen. They run the numbers and base their decisions solely on mathematics. More power to these people, but I would never do that. Call me a woman who relies on God's leading, intuition, and how I feel about a property, but I'll always personally examine and consider an investment for myself, even if it means I'm trudging through a field wearing my mud boots. If something feels wrong, I run—no explanation needed (although better shoes are preferred when running's involved!).

Another area of consideration for Proven was the state of the family finances. She considers whether she can purchase property and make improvements to it without endangering her family's welfare—and that's tricky. And though the verse mentions only her part in considering the field and buying it, I believe you should never make any sort of major investment decision without also having the consideration of your spouse and any others who are significantly affected or involved. Perhaps Proven was capable and respected enough by her husband to make these decisions on her own. In his heart, he trusted her. That's her, and I'm me. I like some feedback. My husband and I handle different areas of responsibility for our family, but if John, my husband, is absolutely against an investment, we don't do it. Period.

Consideration involves time—taking time to think. In *Women, Men and Money*, William Francis Devine Jr. says that acting deliberately is one of the keys to making a profit. We must make slow, calculated movements—something that goes against our culture. The idea of making progress by slowing down may at first seem out of touch and unreasonable. After all, the world of money is defined by speed—the sale that ends Saturday, or the market that's taking off today with no promise of tomorrow. But Devine counsels that moving deliberately with money helps you make sure you and your partner are in sync, thus eliminating confusion and maintaining your peace of mind while putting cash in the bank.

Another financial adviser I've interviewed believes women, in comparison to men, are generally careful and thorough when making financial decisions, being more research-oriented and less likely to act impulsively or overestimate their level of confidence in decision making. Good for us, especially when we don't succumb to society and salesmen telling us to buy now, think later. Good for us, when we listen to that still, small voice telling us to slow down and really consider the matter before us.

Can you humbly admit that you don't have all the answers?

This is where not knowing everything can come in handy. Reflection requires a humble attitude and also the admission that we don't have all the answers. Before you enter into any investment, remember the Proverbs 31 woman and take time to consider. It's okay to say, "I'm not sure," or "I need more time," or "I'll think about it and get back to you." If the person asking you to invest has a problem with you considering your options, that's a good indication you need to move on. Find advisers who will respect your need to reflect, observe, and understand, and who will honor your intention to weigh every decision and take every thought before God.

Action Application

For the next week, don't rush to make any decision. Take time to *consider*—and observe what this feels like. Take time to write down your thoughts and feelings.

> Be careful how you think; your life is shaped by your thoughts. (Proverbs 4:23, TEV)

INVEST IN YOUR EDUCATION

To be good stewards of our money we must invest time to educate ourselves financially.

As I've mentioned, I work on a magazine-style program for women aired on ABC Family Channel and produced by the Christian Broadcasting Network. Our managing producer for the *Living the Life* program, Julie Jenney, summed it up well one day when she said, "Isn't it amazing? We are given virtually no education for three of the most important things in life: marriage, parenting, and finances."

I joined CBN during "Prayer Week," when we would meet at noon for an hour to worship God and pray for viewers' requests sent in from across the nation. Every single prayer request I was given expressed a desperate need for help with finances. One person made a plea for guidance, one hoped to get out of debt, and another dealt with the debilitating feeling of having no control over money.

God could miraculously solve all these problems for us. Money might suddenly fall from the sky, or we could win the

God expects us to become educated in how to manage money.

lottery tomorrow. God could make that happen...but, more than likely, He won't. He expects us to do our job to become educated in how to manage money and invest wisely. We need to be good stewards. Then He expects us to take action, as did Proven as well as the good servants in the Parable of the Talents. God expects us to bring our cares before Him, and He will slowly guide and direct us in how to get a grip on our finances.

To honestly bring our finances into the light is one of the most frightening things we can do. But it's the only way. We can bury our heads in the sand for only so long before we begin to suffocate. And remember, God is working *for* you, not against you!

Meeting Robert Kiyosaki, author of *Rich Dad, Poor Dad*, forced me to realize how my college degrees that looked good on paper would never pay the bills for me. We're taught virtually nothing about how to handle our money in school. We aren't taught to read a financial statement or even to balance our own checkbooks. And I was a business major!

For most of my life I could relate to the poor dad in Kiyosaki's book—highly educated but financially broke. Even with my Christian upbringing, my family sure didn't talk about money much, unless it was to complain about how little we had. At first I felt angry when I realized I had to begin my education again, this time with a different focus: to learn what worked for the long term—in fact, what worked, period! What I found brought me back to the beginning, the Word of God. To the Author and Provider of all the financial models and resources we'll ever need.

I spent two years investing in educating myself about real

estate principles, practices, law, finance, and appraisal before I ever invested in income-producing property. No time for anything like that, you say? In a production meeting for the program *Living the Life*, prior to one of my financial segments on women and investing, one of the other women said, "My problem is, I don't have time to learn about investing…not with children and a job!" My response was this: You don't have to know everything about investing; you just have to understand your "field," as Proven did. She was a real estate investor, and she gave herself time and consideration to understand her strategy.

> Start paying attention to the financial world around you.

Likewise, if you choose to invest in stocks and bonds as your "field," spend time learning the game. An education is needed here as well, because according to Andrew Tobias, author of *The Only Investment Guide You'll Ever Need*, about 90 percent of the people who play the commodities game get burned.[4] He convinced me.

So how do you find your field? Start walking. Begin paying attention to the financial world around you and especially to those investments that work for the long term. So many opportunities exist today to learn: from watching financial news channels to attending a seminar; from reading a book on money to joining an investment club that turns education into action. You don't have to spend a great deal of time on this. Perhaps you can start with just fifteen minutes, three days a week.

Who has time to learn about investing? You do! Because managing money is something you'll always have to deal with while you're on this earth. Always. Unless you have a trust fund the size of Trump Tower, you'll have to face this. You'll feel frightened and overwhelmed at first, thinking "I can never do this," but keep going. Keep learning. With Christ, nothing is insurmountable.

Action Application

What are three ways you can begin to learn about finances and find your field of investment?

Pick just one of those ways, and crack open the books for just fifteen minutes, three days a week. That's less than an hour per week for information that can change the rest of your life. You can't afford to be too busy.

My God will supply all your needs according to His riches in glory in Christ Jesus. (Philippians 4:19)

AVOID GET-RICH-QUICK SCHEMES

One year I ordered a tape and workbook series on investing. Within a month, I began getting solicitations from every get-rich-quick guru on the planet. (Don't you love it when they sell your name and address?) "Make money without lifting a finger!" "Let us put money into your bank account every month!" "Learn the secrets of the rich by sending just $29.99!" Yeah, right. They were obviously overlooking Solomon's counsel:

Dishonest money dwindles away, but he who gathers money little by little makes it grow. (Proverbs 13:11, NIV)

Little by little is the key—not schemes for instant wealth.

At the time I received those mailers, I was working as a reporter for an NBC affiliate station, and every solicitation I got went straight into the hands of the producer for our investigative unit. Those things rarely work! I knew not to fall for any of those outrageous offers. How did I know? Because my husband and I had already been taken for thousands of dollars once before.

A dear friend (you know what they say about friends and business) who was well known and respected in the community was approached by a man who promised big bucks for little effort. We listened to his pitch on a web-based business that was "guaranteed" to quickly make thousands of extra dollars in income every month.

As I was listening to the pitch, somehow I knew he was a fraud. Every cell in my body was screaming for me to exit the room…now! The Holy Spirit within me was all but shouting, "Run, stupid!" (Just kidding; God doesn't usually call us stupid.) But I wanted to be nice and polite. I didn't want to offend anyone or make a friend uncomfortable by walking out. So we stayed and heard it all. We invested the money—then never saw the guy again, or the big bucks he promised.

Tough lesson. And so unnecessary, because God had tried to save us from our idiocy.

Jesus once said,

> "Wealth from get-rich-quick schemes quickly disappears; wealth from hard work grows."
> (Proverbs 13:11 NLT)

"Behold, I send you out as sheep in the midst of wolves;
so be shrewd as serpents and innocent as doves."
(Matthew 10:16)

These words were directed at His twelve disciples as He sent them into the world specifically to preach the gospel. But I believe this truth is applicable on every level of our lives. Be wise. Be shrewd.

And here's the reality check: Not everyone has your best interest at heart. Do I really have to tell you that? Yes, I think I do, because I've found that in the area of finances, women can be way too trusting.

Research conducted by an investment firm I once did business with suggested that women are more inclined than men to place a high value on trust and to remain loyal to investment professionals. But that trust and loyalty can be misplaced, as I've learned to my dismay and by the loss of thousands of dollars. We can hold on to relationships we've built even when it's causing money to disappear before our eyes.

> It's our responsibility to be wise, shrewd, and creative with our money.

The investment company that conducted this research also published a marketing strategy for brokers to capitalize on developing relationships based on women's trust. That's fine when the brokers are trustworthy, but many aren't.

If an investment strategy isn't working for you, get out. Get out now, before you lose even more money. Yes, I know—you don't want to offend anyone. You don't want people to think you're a pain in the neck. You want people to like you. Great! So join a gardening club or an exercise group. Join a charity fund-raising organization. Just don't mess around with your money. Your account manager may tell you things like, "Hey, I'm the expert here. Just trust me." But *you* have the ultimate responsibility to manage your money.

God cares what kind of manager you are. Consider this story that Jesus told:

> There was a rich man who had a manager. Some said that the manager was wasting what the rich man owned. So the rich man told him to come in. He asked him, "What is this I hear about you? Tell me exactly how you have handled what I own. You can't be my manager any longer."
>
> The manager said to himself, "What will I do now? My master is taking away my job. I'm not strong enough to dig. And I'm too ashamed to beg. I know what I'm going to do. I'll do something so that when I lose my job here, people will welcome me into their houses."
>
> So he called in each person who owed his master something. He asked the first one, "How much do you owe my master?"
>
> "I owe 800 gallons of olive oil," he replied.
>
> The manager told him, "Take your bill. Sit down quickly and change it to 400 gallons."
>
> Then he asked the second one, "And how much do you owe?"
>
> "I owe 1,000 bushels of wheat," he replied.

The manager told him, "Take your bill and change it to 800 bushels."

The manager had not been honest. But the master praised him for being clever. (Luke 16:1–8, NIrV)

What do you think of this passage? Should this manager be rewarded or fired? I can make a good argument for either. What was praised in this passage is the manager's ingenuity, not his dishonesty. Likewise, it's our responsibility to be wise, shrewd, and even creative with our money.

Creating wealth in your life isn't easy. It takes time and it takes consideration. If my husband and I had taken time to truly "consider" that field—the investment opportunity that our friend brought our way—we definitely wouldn't have bought it. It taught us a lesson about the danger of "being nice." God expects us to use wisdom in making our financial decision, not to hand over money because we don't want to offend anyone.

The next time a dear friend, family member, neighbor, or anyone else approaches you with a deal that sounds too good to be true, know that it is. Listen to the Holy Spirit telling you to run. Then run!

Action Application

List three ways you can begin to make your money grow, little by little.

Now pick one of those ways and take a step to begin learning

more. Ask God for guidance, and know that you'll receive it in the
right time.

Remember that you aren't alone in this, as Jesus promised:

"The Helper, the Holy Spirit, whom the Father will
send in My name, He will teach you all things, and
bring to your remembrance all that I said to you. Peace
I leave with you; My peace I give to you; not as the
world gives do I give to you. Do not let your heart be
troubled, nor let it be fearful." (John 14:26–27)

IF YOU DON'T UNDERSTAND IT, DON'T DO IT

Another reason we should have run from the get-rich-quick
deal brought to us by a friend is that neither my husband nor I
really understood it. The salesman spoke a mile a minute, making very little sense. When he compared his story to that of Bill
Gates, which should have been red flag number one, the
reporter in me couldn't resist the urge to question him about
this. But he took my question as a personal affront and insinu-
ated that all this investment stuff was really over my head
anyway. I shut my mouth for the remainder of the meeting.
Another bad move and another lesson to be learned.

Make sure you
have a basic
understanding of
what you're
putting your
money into.

One of my investment rules to live by was echoed by an
investment counselor I interviewed for the *Living the Life* program. Doreen Roadman, of JJ Schopen & Associates in Virginia
Beach, expressed it simply: "If you don't understand it, don't do
it." Smart lady. But putting her words into practice takes
humility.

Many of us have a hard time admitting we don't know everything or have all the answers. Losing lots of money has all but cured me of the disease of arrogance. I would much rather admit I don't understand an investment and have someone think I'm stupid than actually prove them right by losing my money.

Consider your field, just as Proven did. Weigh all the benefits and downfalls objectively. Take time, seek information, and evaluate it carefully until you have at least a basic understanding of what you're putting your money into.

I mentioned earlier that I took two years learning about real estate before I actually bought my first "field." As we signed the first contract for our first investment property, I almost backed out, thinking I just didn't know enough yet. Thankfully, God gave me the courage to go ahead with it, and it was truly the best financial investment we've ever made. I still don't know everything about my chosen method of investment, but I know enough to understand what I'm signing. I also know now to be humble enough to admit when I don't get it.

Pride goes before destruction, and a haughty spirit before stumbling. (Proverbs 16:18)

Think of it this way: When you're humble, you're less likely to stumble.

Action Application

Acknowledge and write down three things you don't know about investing. Just three questions.

This week, find the answers. Ask until you get *thorough* responses.

> The heart of the discerning acquires knowledge; the ears
> of the wise seek it out. (Proverbs 18:15, NIV)

ASK THE DUMB QUESTIONS

And how should you word those questions you have about investing? The answer is: Express them any way you want. Don't worry about what you sound like. Asking dumb questions is an area in which I have much experience, after almost eighteen years of reporting. Humbling questions. Questions like, "What does that mean?" As dumb as it might sound, such a question can capture and elicit the most substantial and important information.

It's *your* money on the line—so ask the questions that no one else will.

One of the biblical principles I used to have the hardest time applying in my life as a young woman was this:

> Therefore humble yourselves under the mighty hand of
> God, that He may exalt you at the proper time. (1 Peter 5:6)

As an inexperienced reporter, I thought I was always supposed to look smart and appear as if I had it all together. Now I realize that a true professional is humble, admitting when she doesn't know all the answers.

> A man's pride will bring him low, but a humble spirit
> will obtain honor. (Proverbs 29:23)

Who cares if somebody thinks you're ignorant? Why should you care what others think when it's *your* money on the line, not theirs? So ask the questions about investing that no one else will dare ask.

At times you'll get condescending looks and answers; I guarantee it, because I have. But ask anyway, because it's your money and your responsibility. And keep asking until you get an answer that makes sense to you. To "consider" your field of investment, you have to examine it, and no inquiry is off-limits.

One of my favorite people I've had the pleasure to interview is Herb Cohen, a master negotiator and author of *Negotiate This! By Caring, But Not T-H-A-T Much.* As a negotiator, he has worked with top-level government agencies, all the while preserving his razor-sharp sense of humor. He has taught me that in negotiations, "speed kills." One of his favorite words is, "Huh?" We should actually train ourselves to say such responses as, "I don't know," "I don't understand," "Gee, I'm sorry, you lost me," "Could you please repeat that?" and "Where are we?" His advice is to "slow down, control your response and tread softly....Teach yourself to dwell amidst silence and ambiguity."[5] How tough is that?

As a young reporter, I felt I had to fill every moment of silence. I didn't want to make the other person feel uncomfortable or awkward. Now I don't care. Well, I care, but not *t-h-a-t* much. Thanks, Herb.

Action Application

In considering an investment that someone is promoting to you, here are a few questions to get answers for:

- Does this person make the majority of his or her money in what they're advising you to invest in?

- What are his financial incentives? Does he have a quota to meet?

- Is he a person of integrity, and can he back up his trustworthiness with references?

- What does he have to show to support what he's saying?

Remember, Jesus says we'll know people by their "fruits." Their character traits will be made evident through their actions and accomplishments—what they produce in their lives. So ask for evidence of results.

INFORMATION, NOT IMAGINATION

Have you ever had an important decision to make, so important that you began imagining the worst that could happen? Before you knew it, your imagination got the best of you and you talked yourself out of an opportunity that could have been exceptional. You let fear get the best of you.

As a younger woman, making important decisions was one of the most arduous, wearisome challenges I had to conquer. I was afraid of making the wrong decision, so many times I made no decision at all. Or I would delegate the decision to someone else, calling friends or family saying, "What should I do?" Then I would do nothing. Sound familiar?

The "wicked, lazy slave" in Jesus' Parable of the Talents also understood this type of immobilizing cowardice. Not to beat up on this guy, but listen to his answer when his master questioned him as to why he didn't invest the money:

> "Master, I knew you to be a hard man, reaping where you did not sow and gathering where you scattered no seed. And I was afraid, and went away and hid your talent in the ground. See, you have what is yours." (Matthew 25:24–25)

Pray, put aside speculation, and base your decision on *information*.

This servant let his imagination and fear overwhelm his ability to reason. As a result, he did nothing. As the master in the story later reminded him, he should have at least put the money in the bank for a small return, given the information he had. Instead, the slave let his fear of a tough master overtake him.

Proven was the polar opposite of this lazy slave. She took her time in gathering information, she scrutinized and contemplated that information, and then she acted upon it, not letting fear get in her way.

"She considers a field and buys it; from her earnings she plants a vineyard" (Proverbs 31:16). Her example is echoed in a lesson I was taught in the middle of a difficult and confusing negotiation process. The rational and immeasurably wise attorney who was helping me with the contract told me to always base my decisions on *information*, not imagination.

This is so difficult to do, because it involves taking control of our thoughts. But God understands when you and I are afraid.

Remember, we have an advocate in Jesus Christ. Therefore we

can "demolish arguments [or *speculations*, as in the *New American Standard Bible*] and every pretension that sets itself up against the knowledge of God," and we can "take captive every thought to make it obedient to Christ" (2 Corinthians 10:5, NIV).

This is great advice for every area of our lives, including our finances. Put aside speculations and imaginations, pray about your challenges and opportunities, and then base your decisions on information. Don't let fear make your decisions for you.

> For you have not received a spirit of slavery leading to fear again, but you have received a spirit of adoption as sons by which we cry out, "Abba! Father!" (Romans 8:15)

Action Application

Make a decision today based on information, not imagination. Based on facts, not fear.

Write out the pros and cons of the consequences of this decision, and consider them. Ask for God's help in your evaluation.

When you've considered the information, make your decision and act upon it. Then let it go. Don't worry about it anymore.

LEARN THE LANGUAGE

In the field of television news we have our own language, as you probably do in your job. A story might be called a "package." We refer to copy with video over it as a "voice-over" or "V-O." An interview clip is a "sound bite" or "sound on tape" ("SOT").

Very simply, if a TV news reporter doesn't know this language, she can't do her job. If her boss said, "We need a package for six [o'clock] and a VO-SOT for five," she'd better understand what he's asking for, or she won't be around long.

The same principle applies to investing; if you don't understand the language, you're history…or at least your money is. This is so critical to your success!

Before I ever began investing in real estate, I took the time to learn the language of the field. It seemed overwhelming at first, but as I continued to learn, I also realized that I was dealing merely with words. If I could understand the words and the language of investing, then I could understand the principles, which I could then apply to building wealth and multiplying my own "talents."

In the back of this book I've included several appendices as a reference for you in beginning to invest. While not comprehensive, they're a good start. I've focused on key words in the language of real estate, market investment, and estate planning, to keep things simple. Don't underestimate the importance of learning the words you'll use to grow your money. Certainly, as Proven was considering her field of investment, she also had to take time to understand the language that would eventually help her buy that field.

> First understand the words…and then you'll come to understand the principles.

If you're at all like me, learning a new language seems difficult and scary. When I first started watching CNBC, business degree in hand, I kept thinking, *They're speaking too fast* and *I don't understand a word they're saying.* Slowly I began to get it. It's a game, and I had to learn the rules. Consider investing as a game, because it will make it much more fun. Learn the rules of your chosen game before you create your strategy to win it.

Action Application

Take fifteen minutes, three days a week, to specifically concentrate on the language of investing. Read the financial page of your newspaper or listen to a report on a business network. It will all look and sound like gibberish to you at first, but don't stop. It will start to make sense, one word at a time.

> The beginning of wisdom is: Acquire wisdom; and with all your acquiring, get understanding. (Proverbs 4:7)

Part III

INVEST

CHAPTER FOUR

Time to Buy the Field

I mentioned earlier that when I first read Proverbs 31 as a young woman, I had no clue what this lady was up to, especially the part about a vineyard. Why a vineyard? Didn't she have enough on her plate taking care of her family and giving back to her community? Weren't her entrepreneurial efforts in making clothes and belts enough to keep her occupied? Why in the world would she want to add a vineyard to the mix of her multiple responsibilities?

The answer: Proven found it important not only to spend her time working for money but also to make her money eventually work for her. Someday in the future, as she grew older, her hands wouldn't be able to "grasp the spindle" (v. 19) as she once had. As a senior citizen she might not be able to put her hands to work creating linen garments. She needed to find a source of "passive income" for her family—that is, an investment that would provide money whether she showed up to work every day or not. (Active income requires our continuous direct involvement—as in a daily nine-to-five job, for example.

But passive or residual income represents all investments that generate revenue without that continuous involvement.)

Here's an interesting fact about vineyards: I've read that a single vine, with proper care, can bear as much as eighty pounds of grapes yearly for as long as a century, providing a crop each year for table grapes, wine, raisins, or various other uses. Talk about a long-term investment! Proven's vineyard could provide a significant source of income for her and her family both now and in the future. She was producing a stream of income with multiple products and little waste.

I think Proven was stunningly capable and clever in making such a wise, multiple-use, long-term investment. We can follow her example today in our own unique ways. Let's consider some possibilities.

Action Application

Take a few moments to brainstorm about different products that can be useful in today's society and that can also provide you and your family with a source of passive income. Get creative! Remember what it was like to think like a child when nothing was impossible—"For nothing is impossible with God" (Luke 1:37, NIV).

THE SEVEN LAWS OF REAL ESTATE INVESTING

For me and my family, investing in real estate is the closest thing to Proven's vineyard in today's financial world. This isn't a get-rich-quick plan where you promptly become a millionaire overnight. This is also not an investment for the faint-hearted or the risk-averse. The housing market will take turns for the better and the worse. Interest rates go up and down. Real estate investment requires a great deal of time spent researching properties and doing your homework on your target market and how to make a property deal work. (In Appendix B, I've given you a few important terms and principles to get you started in a better understanding of real estate investment. Real estate, like every investment, requires more education on your part. You don't need a college degree or a real estate license, but you do need to understand the words and rules of the game.)

> Real estate is not an investment for the faint-hearted or the risk-averse.

Though many real estate advisers say you can begin with a no-money-down deal, I'm wary of this approach. But I believe you can begin with just a few thousand dollars, as my husband and I did, in a careful, methodical approach to acquiring your first property. You can fix it up, rent it, or sell it and begin again to consider other properties to acquire.

As you think about this possibility, consider for a moment what I call the seven laws of real estate investing, seven principles or factors that greatly influence what happens in real estate.

1. The Law of Supply and Demand

Real estate is a proven long-term investment for many reasons.

First and foremost, it involves the simple economic principle of supply and demand. People will always need a place to live and work—and there's only so much land to go around.

Like any investment market, real estate will have its ups and downs, reflecting general economic conditions. But in the long run, well-located real estate in most cases will endure these fluctuations and appreciate in value.

2. The Law of Creativity

As we keep in mind Proven's example of creativity, we can definitely view real estate as one of the most creative forms of investment in and of itself. You can invest for the long term by holding property and renting it, or you can become a short-term investor by fixing up distressed properties and then quickly reselling them. You can work on your own or with partners, corporations, or limited liability companies. You can invest in a range of property types from town homes and single family homes to commercial buildings and all the way to land speculation, depending upon your entrepreneurial, adventuresome spirit. You can also own a piece of the pie through a Real Estate Investment Trust (REIT), a mutual fund with real property assets or mortgages (debt-based securities). While the property available is limited by the law of supply and demand, the creative potential of real estate investing is limitless.

> The creative potential of real estate investing is limitless.

3. The Law of Consideration

In *The Complete Idiot's Guide to Real Estate Investing*, Stuart Leland Rider reminds us that while anyone can make a good living by working hard and getting a decent education, if you want more than just a good living, you must take risks.

Isn't that exactly what Proven did for her family's financial life? It wasn't enough for her to just create and sell wonderful linen clothing or belts for the tradesmen. She took it to the next level by using her income to make a wise real estate investment and planting a vineyard that would feed her family for generations to come.

Her vineyard investment could have been a flop. A drought, hailstorm, or locust infestation could have damaged or killed the vines. Proven considered those risks. But she faced them in light of her God-given, multiple talents, which she refused to bury in the sand.

Property forces you to use your mind by taking such calculated risks, and by using careful "consideration," just as Proven did.

4. The Law of OPM

OPM means "other people's money." The really great thing about real estate investing is that you don't have to be rich to do it, because you can use other people's money to buy your investment for you.

This is also known as the law of leverage or financing. Jerry Fung's *Real Estate Principles* describes leverage as using a small amount of your money (equity capital) and a large amount of someone else's money (borrowed money) to buy real estate. He cautions that leverage works only if the property increases in value. So consider your location well and thoroughly.

The most successful businesspeople know how to capitalize on the power of leveraging.

5. The Law of OPT

OPT means "other people's time." Proven's vineyard would require someone's supervision and care, and your real estate investment will require the same—either from you or from others whom you hire.

Experienced, competent property managers can supervise your property for you. Many real estate advisers recommend that you manage whatever property you decide to purchase yourself. That's wonderful if you don't already have a full-time job, not to mention a full-time family.

Many people say this is the reason they wouldn't even consider real estate as an investment; they don't want to get phone calls about leaky toilets in the middle of the night. I don't either! Who does? But property managers are paid to take those calls for you, whether they like it or not. Yes, they will also take an average of 10 percent of your profit, and more for resort property. So you'll have to decide whether your time and peace of mind are worth that expense. Compare that 10 percent cost to the return you can reasonably expect on your investment. In many cases, the return is well worth the fee.

When Proven considered her field of dreams and purchased it, I doubt the field was right next door. That wouldn't have taken much consideration. But she could hardly have left her home for extended hours each day to take care of things at her vineyard while she also raised children, managed her helpers, worked in the community, and ran another business making belts and clothing. My humble opinion is that just as she had help around the house, she also had a manager for her vineyard.

6. The Law of Passive Income

We looked earlier at how important passive or residual income can be to a secure financial future. Let me appeal to you on a different level. Remember when, as a child, you'd just had a rotten day at school? Maybe you got into a fight with your best friend, or you spilled paint on your best dress and your mom was angry with you. Don't you wish you could go back and just give yourself a hug, telling your younger self that everything would be okay?

Now imagine yourself as a senior citizen. Have you ever done this before? Have you really considered who and where you'll be when you're older? Picture yourself at seventy years old. Your children are married and have their own families. Your savings doesn't quite cover your health care costs and all the prescription drugs you need. You really wish you had extra money to travel, the way you'd always planned to do in your golden years.

Now is your chance to give your older self a hug—a financial hug—by planning for the future. Now! Now, when you're able to work. Now, when you're able to think creatively. Someday, when you're no longer able to work every day for an income, when Social Security may or may not be there, when your 401(k) account is dwindling, you absolutely must have an investment that will provide income month after month.

As I've stressed, real estate investing isn't for everyone. You either love it or you don't. The investors I've met who are truly successful absolutely love the business. It just might be the right "vineyard" for you too.

7. The Law of Tax Advantage

Real estate is a relatively unique investment compared to the stock market and other investments because it offers so many tax

> Picture yourself at seventy years old. Really consider who and where you'll be.

benefits. The interest you pay on mortgages for investment property is a write-off at tax time. Can you do that with your antiques or your stamp collection? You can refinance your property without taking a tax hit. You can exchange your property (1031 tax-deferred exchange), allowing you to take on larger, potentially better deals. There are other tax incentives as well.

In no way is this book intended to offer legal or tax advice. My intent is to highlight Proven's investment plan, as she also bought real estate. I want to get you thinking about your own field of investment. There are thousands of real estate investing resources and books available today and a countless number of creative approaches and perspectives on this financial resource.

We must also remember who holds the true title to our property: "The earth is the LORD's, and all it contains, the world, and those who dwell in it" (Psalm 24:1). We're simply the tenants, while God is the Landlord. On the day you pay off that thirty-year mortgage, you must also realize that God is the real owner of your property. That doesn't mean having a casual or uncaring attitude. It means we have a responsibility to go over and above what's merely adequate in taking care of our investments. In our hearts, we should make a transfer of our possessions to God, while in our actions, we should strive for excellence in managing them.

Action Application

Think about how you feel when you consider investing in real estate. Is it a sense of fear or a sense of empowerment?

Remember: God holds the true "title" to all our property.

Take your concerns to God in prayer and see the answers He will provide. Remember, real estate may or may not be your "field."

As you think about this, consider the true source of power:

O Lord, You have great power, shining-greatness and strength. Yes, everything in heaven and on earth belongs to You. You are the King, O Lord. And You are honored as head over all. Both riches and honor come from You. You rule over all. Power and strength are in Your hand. The power is in Your hand to make great and to give strength to all. (1 Chronicles 29:11–12, NLV)

YOUR BUSINESS

Not only did Proven have the mind of an investor; she also built her financial foundation with the mind of an entrepreneur.

Proven reminds me of the many stunningly capable businesswomen I had opportunity to interview and work with during my years as a reporter. In Colorado Springs, I hosted a national program on the Business Radio Network called *Women Talk Business*. The program was sponsored by the National Association of Women Business Owners, a group of entrepreneurs from whom I began to learn lessons that would change the way I viewed work.

On *Living the Life*, I profiled another small group that calls itself "Not Your Average Housewives." Many of the ladies are

stay-at-home moms who have become business owners and
investors instead of getting a full-time job outside the home.
(Does this sound like Proverbs 31 to you?) This association also
teaches that business ownership allows for much more freedom,
opportunity, and control over your work, not to mention tax
benefits. It allows you to realize you always have options and
you never have to settle for a job you don't love.

Build your financial
foundation with
the mind of an
entrepreneur.

For young moms with tiny babies, owning a business
allows them time with their children. One investor gave me a
tour of a house she was rehabilitating, and she carried her baby
the entire time she showed me around the place. While I was
so happy for her, I was also sad for myself. When I was a young
mom with little babies, I hadn't learned to apply the lessons of
the Proverbs 31 woman, and I was nowhere near taking control of my work life. Thankfully, as our children have grown
older, I've learned to apply Proven's lessons to my own life: to
create, consider, and invest. It was for freedom that Christ set
us free (Galatians 5:1), and I believe He intended us to have
freedom in every way, if we'll grasp it.

In her study guide to Proverbs 31, Eleanor Reid notes that
people often equate business with large operations, which not
everyone has the ability and the talent to run. However, a vast
variety of businesses can be run out of our own homes with
only one person as an employee, as opposed to a more typical
business requiring office and manufacturing space.[6] The truth
is that you really can own your own business. And as an entrepreneur, you'll gain the freedom to make decisions, along with
greater flexibility with your schedule.

Action Application

List the hobbies you love that could potentially become your own business. Stuff you love. The things you'll do anyway, regardless of whether you make a profit.

Recall the description of Proven—that she "works with her hands *in delight*" (Proverbs 31:13). What brings you delight in your life?

INTELLECTUAL PROPERTY

Einstein once spoke of imagination as being more important than knowledge. Proven used her imagination often, whether it was to choose the best material for making quality clothes and belts or actually designing a fabric's pattern. Today we can also use our minds to create intellectual property that can be recognized and protected by patents, copyrights, and trademarks. It's important to protect your ideas so you don't lose your rights and your profits.

Are you a creative person with lots of ideas?

You've probably heard of Wally Amos of Famous Amos Cookies, "the face that launched a thousand chips." The Famous Amos cookie tale began when Wally, a talent agent, began using his bite-sized cookies as calling cards. At the urging of his friends and clients, he launched the Famous Amos Cookie Company in 1975 in a Sunset Boulevard storefront in Hollywood. The business grew, and in 1985, Famous Amos Cookies was a $10 million business.

Years later he came for an interview at a news station where I worked, but he wasn't promoting his cookies. He was promoting muffins without his well-known name. He also gave me a copy of his book, *Turn Lemons into Lemonade*, about turning adverse situations into opportunities. He wrote the book after losing his company, then watching it get sold for $63 million without his receiving any of the proceeds. He hadn't protected the rights to his name, and the company he founded took control over ownership of his name and likeness. But with the spirit of a true survivor, Wally was determined to bounce back, to turn lemons into lemonade, and to keep moving forward as someone other than "Famous Amos."

At an investment seminar, I met Michael Lechter, a lawyer who has written a book called *Protecting Your #1 Asset: Creating Fortunes from Your Ideas*. In it he writes that intellectual property is to the world of business what the Colt .45 was to the dime-novel old West—the great equalizer. It's the thing that permits a small, startup business to compete against larger, better established competitors.[7]

At the most basic level, intellectual property includes anything that can be protected by copyrights, patents, and trademarks. In today's business world, intellectual property can range from information regarding technology to the collective knowledge of a company or an individual in that company. Even if you never plan to compete with the big boys, consider protecting the creation of your ideas by first doing research through the U.S. Patent and Trademark Office (www.uspto.gov) or the U.S. Copyright Office (www.copyright.gov), then contacting an attorney who specializes in intellectual property. If you're a creative person with lots of ideas, this may become your Proven field of investment.

Action Application

I've always marveled at the creativity of God. He's a true artist, full of ideas that He accomplished with a word.

Today is *your* day to think creatively. What will it be: As an artist? An author? An entrepreneur?

List three ideas you have which could be considered intellectual property. If you believe one of these ideas is your field of investment, take action to protect it.

God saw everything he had made. And it was very good. (Genesis 1:31, NIrV)

PAPER ASSETS

Shortly after the stock market plunge following the Enron and WorldCom scandals, curious signs began appearing at fast-food restaurants—signs with pictures of elderly people wearing forced smiles and a caption touting the joys of earning extra income during your golden years. Ouch. My heart hurt for the countless Americans who lost their shirts, not to mention their retirement funds, as they watched their paper assets evaporate with every developing story of corporate corruption.

Two forces drive the stock market: greed and fear.

For reporters, this was a headline. For our senior citizens, it was a catastrophe. For those who relied on the stock market to secure their future, this should have been a lesson.

Playing the stock market can be valuable for giving us experience in managing the two forces that have always driven the markets from the Great Depression to the new millennium:

greed and fear. I've known both the temptation of greed when my stock picks soar and the immobilizing phenomenon of fear as I watch my chosen company's stock price plummet, along with my investment. While I worked in news during the booming nineties, several colleagues and I loved to play the stock market and exchange "hot" stock tips. It was great fun until the bottom dropped out and fear took over. But there was a poignant lesson in losing thousands of dollars. I learned that failure didn't kill me. But I was still young enough to have time for mistakes, unlike my senior neighbors.

Once again, we're talking about numbers, which go up and down. Truly, if you're planning to invest in the stock market, failure will be part of the game. Dealing with paper assets is a game and a gamble. When you invest in the markets, you're investing in someone else's company, management style, and accounting practices, as well as their vision, expertise, and ethics—or lack thereof. You have absolutely no control over your investment. And if you hire a broker to make your picks for you, you have even less influence.

Does this sound like an investment Proven would make? That's a question you'll have to answer for yourself, and your answer may well differ from mine. God gives us all our own investment styles. However, if you choose to invest in the stock market, you'll have to learn to manage your emotions even more than managing dollars.

Most stock market investors end up buying high and selling low.

Spend time considering this field from all angles. (As a start for learning what you need to know of the language and rules of the stock market game, see Appendix C.) You'll discover your own investment methods and styles once you begin. If you choose to play the market, learn the rules of the game before you start. And watch the market. One way to begin tracking the movement of the markets is to follow a price index such as the Standard & Poor's S&P 500, which includes five hundred stocks in its average, providing a broad view of current trends in the stock market. The S&P 500 measures top firms in all the leading industries, including retail, auto, chemical, banking, and technology. (The Dow Jones Industrial Average is another popular indicator of market change, but this index contains only thirty representative stocks.)

In *Profit from the Evening News*, Marie Bussing-Burks comments on watching the S&P 500 in considering the best time to buy stocks:

> The S&P hits its high point an average of six months prior to a recession. The index and its representative stocks fall during the recession as investors become skeptical about the economy's performance and sell their stocks. Selling puts downward pressure on stock prices. This is the best time to be buying stocks, because if the S&P is down, it's likely the stocks you're interested in are down as well.[8]

Think of it as bargain shopping: Buy low, sell high. Unfortunately, most investors end up doing just the opposite—buying high and selling low.

Investment advisers have noted how many people feel more confident, and thus invest more, when prices are high, just as they feel more pessimistic and are tempted to sell when prices are low.[9] The first step to managing your paper assets is to realize that this buy-high, sell-low syndrome can happen to you.

One research firm has noted that from 1984 to 2002, the average stock mutual fund racked up returns averaging 10.2 percent a year, while average investors made only 2.6 percent a year because they didn't hang on through thick and thin. This means that an investment of $10,000 in a typical fund should have grown to $63,600 during that time, but instead the average investor's portfolio grew to only $16,300—and actually declined in value once inflation is taken into account.

So watch out for the pitfalls, do your homework, and try to gain a feel for the market and your ability to predict trends. It will take research, time, and self-control. It will take time to *consider.*

Action Application

Begin learning about the different paper assets available to you.

Assess your risk level. Are you willing to be more aggressive with the funds you invest, or will you tend to be more conservative?

Consider opening a small brokerage account with money you aren't afraid to lose. Many online accounts offer great trading prices and informational resources.

Begin doing your own research and making your own decisions about what to buy and sell. Track your own progress for a year.

A wise man will hear and grow in learning. A man of understanding will become able. (Proverbs 1:5, NLV)

SEEK WISE COUNSEL

Unlike most everything else in life, in the world of investing, practice does not make perfect. This game isn't like any sport or craft you've ever encountered. Hours of drills on the playing field or lessons in the classroom do not guarantee success in the real world. Sometimes even professional investment managers cannot outperform a monkey with a handful of darts in choosing stocks. And if a monkey can sometimes invest in paper assets just as competently as the paid professionals, certainly you and I can too. We can take aim and give it a shot. Many financial "experts" as well as laypeople think there's a "trick" or some reliable "secret" to successful investing. They may mean well, but for investing, what you need is wisdom, not opinion or social pressures.

> Practice does not make perfect. You need wisdom from others.

Maybe you're the one person who hasn't been burned by a so-called expert or trusted friend at least once in your life. If so, I'm genuinely happy for you. But sadly, most folks can't share in that blessing when it comes to stock market investment. I allowed myself to be burned twice by the same person, a broker who claimed to be a strong Christian. Apparently losing money with him the first time wasn't enough. He seemed so nice (there's that word again), so I invested with him a second time and again lost thousands of dollars. Please learn from my mistakes and apply three rules I've learned about seeking wise counsel for your investments.

The first rule comes from another author I had a chance to interview, Harvey Mackay, who wrote *Swim with the Sharks Without Being Eaten Alive*. He was in town to promote his latest book, *Pushing the Envelope*, and I'll never forget him. Talk about someone who follows through on his word! After our interview, I told him I would like to read some of his other books; he promptly promised to send me all of them, and to get them to me within forty-eight hours. Sure enough, in less than two days I had a box of books to read and many business lessons to learn.

In *Pushing the Envelope*, Mackay writes this: "One of my favorite investment probes is 'Are you putting your own money in the investment that you're recommending to me?'"[10] Before you invest with anyone, ask that question. Watch for the pause and the discomfort before they say, "Oh, sure…of course." On the other hand, if they immediately and exuberantly say something like, "Absolutely, and it's been the best investment I've ever made," then move on to litmus test number two—which Jesus Himself gave us:

> "Beware of the false prophets, who come to you in sheep's clothing, but inwardly are ravenous wolves. You will know them by their fruits. Grapes are not gathered from thorn bushes nor figs from thistles, are they? So every good tree bears good fruit, but the bad tree bears bad fruit. A good tree cannot produce bad fruit, nor can a bad tree produce good fruit. Every tree that does not bear good fruit is cut down and thrown into the fire. So then, you will know them by their fruits." (Matthew 7:15–20)

You'll know a person by what they produce in their lives. In seeking wise counsel, don't settle just for words. Look for action. Look for the fruit, good and bad.

There's your answer. That is why you should *never* buy anything from brokers who call you up cold. You know nothing about these people! How can you examine their fruit? I also never commit to any financial gift over the phone, unless it's an organization I'm very well acquainted with. I always ask for information in writing, and I ask to see evidence of results.

The third rule of investing in paper assets is to trust God and yourself more than you trust your broker. Ask God for wisdom about financial matters and you'll get answers, if you ask in faith. Brokers—and the firms they represent—simply cannot be trusted in the way God can, and in fact, they are wrong just as often as they're right.

There's an old joke on Wall Street: "The broker made money and the firm made money—and two out of three ain't bad!" So much for the investor!

Investment author Andrew Tobias, in *The Only Investment Guide You'll Ever Need*, tells the story of a firm entrusted with $175,000 to invest in options trading:

> The institution was shrewd in its timing, as it turned out. The stock market rallied dramatically. Never could one have made as much in options as then. Yet in two months, through an elaborate series of computer-assisted ins, outs, and straddles, the firm's options trader managed to turn that $175,000 into

$10,000—generating $87,000 in commissions along the way.[11]

The broker made money, while the investor lost big-time! So consider using a discount broker, or "deep discounter," who makes trading very inexpensive. They won't push you into a sale or hold your hand. Many do, however, provide you with up-to-the-minute research and information so you can make your own decision without rushing into unnecessary trades.

Action Application

In seeking wise counsel for market investment, schedule a face-to-face meeting with a prospective financial expert. It's not enough to just speak to a person over the phone. You'll get a much better feel for this individual in his or her presence, and if something feels wrong, move on with no apologies.

During your meeting, be sure to ask for references. Some financial advisers already have recommendations in writing on a glossy brochure. Fine. But I suggest you also ask for current clients whom you can call personally. It isn't rude to ask for references—after all, this is your money. If he or she is hesitant to provide you with those names, you know what to do: Move on.

Also do this: For just one moment, remember a time when you were burned by a person you thought you could trust. How could applying the above rules have changed that outcome?

Now, forgive that person if you haven't already, and learn from your mistakes. Let it go and move on to your future filled with hope and prosperity.

If any of you lacks wisdom, let him ask of God, who gives to all generously and without reproach, and it will be given to him. But he must ask in faith without any doubting, for the one who doubts is like the surf of the sea, driven and tossed by the wind. (James 1:5–6)

CHAPTER FIVE

Your Personal Numbers (And They Are Just Numbers!)

You have now had some time to think and dream about what life can and will be like if you have faith in the God of all numbers. We talked about investment options because I wanted you to ponder your future before you crunch your own numbers in the present.

Yes, they are just numbers, and God is bigger than all of them. This is the part where we get down and dirty about the reality of our own financial situations. It's time to lift your head from the sand.

But it was so comfortable there, you might be thinking. Yes, I know. It's so much easier to fool ourselves. But we don't have the luxury of blissful ignorance with regard to money—particularly with bills to pay every month. And there's so much to gain from getting your finances under control. Calvin Coolidge once said, "There is no dignity quite so impressive, and no independence quite so important, as living within your means."

So let's take a moment and begin crunching your personal numbers.

You may be cringing inside. Hardly anyone likes to talk about a budget, much less put one down on paper and live by it. In the past, when my financial advisers said the word *budget*, I would tune out completely! Boring. One night I was watching a financial pundit on television suggest that people should write down everything they've spent in the past year, and she told them to "make a date of it with your significant other, a romantic time with a negligee and champagne." Ha! Who was she kidding? If this was the kind of date my husband and I had planned, none of our children would have ever been born.

I thought more about the first part of his suggestion—about creating a budget by reviewing every month's expenses for the past year. Who would actually do that? Isn't it enough to get your tax information together sometime before the April deadline? Imagine dissecting an entire year. On a date, no less!

YOUR BUDGET

I'm going to make this budget process much simpler for you. I want you to look at just two months from the past year. Take your most expensive month—possibly December, during the gift-buying frenzy, or maybe a summer month that includes your family holiday—plus a more normal month, like March, when you don't do as many extra things. Then average your spending for those two months. Voila!—your budget.

Don't lose sight of your dream—of what your life can be if you have faith in the God of all numbers.

So grab your checkbook and get started with the worksheets that follow (no negligee required). Do one worksheet for your most expensive month and another for your least expensive. And yes, include that vacation trip for a couple thousand dollars in your average living cost, because this will help you learn to plan for it instead of relying on MasterCard or Visa. Next vacation, you're paying cash. (Now that's what I call the makings of a real date night!)

Worksheet 1: Expenses (Cash Outflows) for Your Most Expensive Month

Rent/Mortgage Payment	$_____
Auto Expenses	$_____
Food	$_____
Child Care	$_____
Telephone (and Cell Phone)	$_____
Utilities	$_____
Credit Card Payments	$_____
Loan Payments	$_____
Insurance Premiums	$_____
Medical and Dental	$_____
Entertainment (Including Vacations)	$_____
Gifts	$_____
Donations	$_____
House Maintenance	$_____
Other	$_____
Other: _____	$_____
Other: _____	$_____

Total Expenses: $_____

Worksheet 2: Expenses (Cash Outflows) for a Normal Month

Rent/Mortgage Payment $_____

Auto Expenses $_____

Food $_____

Child Care $_____

Telephone (and Cell Phone) $_____

Utilities $_____

Credit Card Payments $_____

Loan Payments $_____

Insurance Premiums $_____

Medical and Dental $_____

Entertainment (Including Vacations) $_____

Gifts $_____

Donations $_____

House Maintenance $_____

Other: _____ $_____

Other: _____ $_____

Other: _____ $_____

Total Expenses: $_____

Worksheet 3: Your General Budget
(The average of expenses for [a] your most expensive month, and [b] a normal month)

Rent/Mortgage Payment $_____

Auto Expenses $_____

Food $_____

Child Care $_____

Telephone (and Cell Phone) $_____

Utilities $_____

Credit Card Payments $_____

Loan Payments $_____

Insurance Premiums $_____

Medical and Dental $_____

Entertainment (Including Vacations) $_____

Gifts $_____

Donations $_____

House Maintenance $_____

Other: _____ $_____

Other: _____ $_____

Other: _____ $_____

Total Expenses: $_____

Now calculate your monthly income. (If this varies from month to month, you will want to follow an averaging procedure similar to the way you determined your monthly expenses.) Use this worksheet:

Worksheet 4: Monthly Income (Cash Inflows)

Net Salary/Wages $_____

(This is after payroll taxes, federal and state taxes, and FICA taxes)

Other Income (dividends) $_____

Rental Income $_____

Gain on Sale of Stocks and Bonds	$_____
Tax Refund	$_____
Gifts or Grants	$_____
Alimony or Child Support	$_____
Other: _____	$_____
Other: _____	$_____
Other: _____	$_____

Total Income: $_____

Now you simply subtract your average monthly expenses from your monthly income to find your monthly surplus (or monthly deficit, if expenses are more than income):

Worksheet 5: Statement of Total Income and Expenses

Total Monthly Income:	$_____
Total Monthly Expenses:	$_____

Surplus (or Deficit) = Income less Expenses: $_____

It's time to lift your head from the sand.

To take managing your money to the next level, take as your starting point the general budget you calculated by using your most and least expensive month. And then, from this month forward, begin tracking your spending. If you're computer savvy, do it through financial software such as Quicken Personal Finance, Microsoft Money, or even Microsoft Excel. If using the computer is too intimidating, stick with the old checkbook, pen, and paper. (That still works for me.)

By the way, how does it feel to be raising your head from the sand? It was getting stuffy down there anyway, wasn't it?

Action Application

As outlined in the instructions above, determine your actual cost of living—your budget—by averaging your most expensive and least expensive months. Figure out your monthly income and your monthly surplus (or deficit) as well.

When you begin this task, you may feel a bit overwhelmed, but keep going. God will help you get a grasp on your personal numbers. And remember: *They're just numbers!*

As you do this budget preparation, keep in mind this story Jesus told:

After a long time the owner of those servants came back. He wanted to know what had been done with his money.

The one who had received the five pieces of money worth much came and handed him five pieces more. He said, "Sir, you gave me five pieces of money. See! I used it and made five more pieces."

His owner said to him, "You have done well. You are a good and faithful servant. You have been faithful over a few things. I will put many things in your care. Come and share my joy."

The one who received two pieces of money worth much came also. He said, "Sir, you gave me two pieces of money. See! I used it and made two more pieces."

His owner said to him, "You have done well. You are

a good and faithful servant. You have been faithful over a few things. I will put many things in your care. Come and share my joy.'" (Matthew 25:19–23, NLV)

MORE NUMBERS THAT MATTER

In considering your field to purchase, you must also consider your debt ratio, or the ratio of your total liabilities to your total assets, and your net worth. All these numbers are particularly important in regard to any money you will want to borrow to finance your "field."

Keep all these numbers in perspective. They *can* be changed and improved.

Your debt ratio indicates to your banker whether you'll be able to repay a mortgage or loan, so it's an important number for you to know. It can be calculated with simple mathematics.

Let's begin by determining your total assets. In the financial world, there's much debate over what an asset is and what a liability is. The authors of *The Complete Idiot's Guide to Beating Debt* try to make it simple. They say an asset makes you money and a liability costs you money.[12] That perspective will come in handy later in this chapter when we talk about getting out of debt. But for your banker, that simple definition doesn't work.

For example, your home costs you tons of money, right? The mortgage must be paid, and there's always something to fix or improve. But in listing your total assets and liabilities, your home is actually an asset, as is your car and any personal property you own. However, any payments you're obligated to make on your home, car, or personal property are classified as liabilities.

When listing your assets, arrange them in order of liquidity, that is, the ability to convert them into cash. For example, you may want to arrange your asset sheet in this order:

Worksheet 6: Your Assets

Cash	$_____
Checking Accounts	$_____
Savings Accounts	$_____
Money Market Funds	$_____
Certificates of Deposit	$_____
Savings Bonds (current value)	$_____
Life Insurance (cash surrender value)	$_____
Annuities (cash surrender value)	$_____
Other Paper Assets—Stocks, Bonds, Mutual Funds	$_____
Market Value of IRA/401(k)/403(b)	$_____
Other Pension Plans	$_____
Market Value of Your Home	$_____
Investment Property	$_____
Automobile	$_____
Household Property	$_____
Jewelry or Other Precious Metals	$_____
Collectibles	$_____
Loan Receivables	$_____
Other	$_____
Total Assets:	**$_____**

Liabilities are the amounts you still owe on your possessions and property—your mortgage, your car payment, installment financing for personal property, and so on. List your liabilities in this way:

Worksheet 7: Your Liabilities

Credit card balances	$_____
Bills outstanding	$_____
Auto loan balances	$_____
Taxes due	$_____
Mortgage loans	$_____
Other	$_____

Total Liabilities: $_____

Your net worth is the difference between the totals of your assets and liabilities.

$$Assets - Liabilities = Net\ Worth$$

For the bank this is an important determinant of a person's overall financial position.

Worksheet 7: Your Net Worth

Total Assets	$_____
Total Liabilities	$_____

Net Worth (Assets less Liabilities): $_____

Your debt ratio, meanwhile, is your total liabilities divided by net worth:

Total Liabilities / Net Worth = Debt Ratio

This is another simple number that means a great deal. Banks will look at your debt ratio in determining your chance for securing financing for homes or businesses.

Worksheet 8: Your Debt Ratio

Total Liabilities	$_____
Net Worth	$_____

Debt Ratio (Liabilities divided by Net Worth): $_____

For example, if you have $100,000 in total liabilities and a net worth of $200,000, your debt ratio would be 0.5.

In general, a debt ratio of 0.5 or less is considered acceptable, whereas a debt ratio greater than 0.5 is considered to be high. A low debt ratio is more appealing to a bank than a high debt ratio because it indicates your greater ability to repay your loan should you encounter financial difficulties.

Ratios and numbers are important to your financial picture. Keep them in perspective, because numbers can be changed and improved.

Action Application

Write out a statement of your personal net worth and determine your debt ratio. This isn't the end of your financial story; it's just the start of extracting your head from the sand.

Take time to thank God for what you have now and for what you will have in the future.

> Give thanks to the LORD, for he is good; his love endures forever. (1 Chronicles 16:34, NIV)

PAPERS TO ORGANIZE

Now that you have a handle on what your personal numbers really look like, take a few hours and get all your papers organized. Think about Proven. There's no way she could have managed her household the way she did, juggling the multiple priorities on her plate, unless she was at least marginally organized.

As I'm writing this, I'm looking around at my desk in my little home office thinking, "Who am I to tell anyone to get organized; there are books and papers everywhere!" I'm not saying we have to be perfect at this. (Part of my to-do list today includes cleaning up my own mess and filing all this stuff—though personally, I'd rather write!)

You need to keep a few basic important papers in a safe, in a filing cabinet, or at least in a notebook. These include:

1. Life insurance policies

2. Homeowner's insurance policy

3. Mortgage information

4. Bank and investment account statements

5. Wills and trusts

6. Tax returns

7. Birth certificates

8. Credit cards paperwork

9. Medical information

10. Retirement and other account statements

Getting organized now *will* pay off in the future.

This list also represents ten areas to get you started in organization. And I know this task looks daunting, but I promise it will pay off in the future when you need to access this information quickly.

It will also pay off in your peace of mind. Smile at the future. Proven did, because she planned for that future and also prepared her financial "house." Proven *cared* about her family and her family's future. Organizing your financial information is one more way you can show your family how much you care and how much you love them.

Action Application

Organize your financial information as described above.

Make sure you tell your husband or beneficiary where everything can be located should they need this information before you do.

As you organize, remember to keep Proven in mind:

She is clothed with strength and dignity; she can laugh
at the days to come. (Proverbs 31:25, NIV)

YOUR CREDIT

Many investors argue that leverage makes real estate a superior
investment. With leverage, you're able to buy a much larger
investment with fewer dollars out of your own pocket because
banks will lend you the rest. In fact, banks and other lending
institutions are actually competing to give you money. Haven't
you seen the huge number of advertisements from lenders? (Most
of these ads focus on loans secured against real estate; you don't
see nearly as many that are associated with any other investment.)

Many real estate investors and advisers say you don't need
good credit to get started in investing. But to that I say,
Baloney! Sure, you can always get someone to loan you
money…but at an exorbitant interest rate with excessive terms
attached to the loan.

So be very careful with your credit. A stronger credit rating
will make investing much cheaper and much less painful. Do
you feel it's too late for that, because you already have bad
credit? Don't get discouraged. It's within your control to raise
your score.

Let's take a look at some of the rules of this credit game.

A credit bureau is an agency that compiles data on an individual's credit history and which will, upon request, distribute a
report on that history to potential creditors. Your rating is based on

a combined score generated from three credit bureaus which look at your credit history, the amount of credit available, and recent inquiries. This information is used to determine what's called your FICO score (FICO is short for "Fair Isaac Corporation," the company that invented this score). It's important to check your score at least once a year. This can determine whether you're eligible to secure a loan and what interest rate you'll pay.

I'm going to put this bluntly: If your credit score is not good, it's a direct result of your past actions and habits—and if your future actions and habits don't change, don't expect to see an improvement in your credit score. But if you take charge of this area of your finances, your credit score can become a powerful tool in your investing.

> If your credit score is *not* good...it's a direct result of your past actions and habits.

For further information on winning the credit game, look at Appendix A, where I've summarized information provided by Kim Pate of Towne Bank Mortgage and Steven Kee of First Point Mortgage Resources in Virginia. It will help you unlock the mysteries of your credit score, how it's determined, how to contact the credit bureaus, and how to report fraud.

For now, here are a few steps to improve your credit score:

1. Pay your bills on time. If you miss a payment, all is not lost. The scoring models all take into account the fact that everyone misses a payment now and then. Also, negative information loses its impact over time; a recent late payment is weighted more heavily than a late payment three or four years ago. It *will* matter if you make on-time payments to rebuild your credit after a period of frequent late

payments, so don't despair. (According to my mort-gage adviser, recent on-time payments account for 35 percent of your score.)

2. Reduce your outstanding debt. Outstanding debt is the amount owed on all credit cards or installment loans. (This category usually determines about 30 percent of your credit score.) Also, to stay in the top rating, make sure to use no more than a third of the credit limit available per account.

Take control…and your credit score can become a powerful tool in your investing.

3. Establish your credit history. Oddly enough, not having any credit is actually worse than having bad credit. If you've never established a credit history, lenders will have no information with which to assess the likelihood that you'll repay their loan. In cases like these, instead of charging a high interest rate, they're more likely to deny the loan altogether. To start your credit history, obtain (and use) at least one credit card, paying it off in full each month. Also try to find a living situation that requires offi-cial monthly rent payments. How long you have had a credit history, how long specific accounts have been established, and how long it has been since you used each account will all tally up to summarize the strength of your credit history. (This category usually determines about 15 percent of your credit score.)

4. Be cautious about pursuing new credit, because this could count against you. The number of new inquiries on your credit, the number of new accounts, and how recent they are can actually count negatively in your credit rating. Too many inquiries are interpreted as a sign that you've been actively seeking credit and may be in financial difficulties. (This category determines about 5 percent of your score.)

5. Be aware of the type of credit used (bank cards, travel and entertainment cards, department store cards, installment loans, etc.), because these can be weighted differently in your score. For example, in some cases, loans from finance companies may negatively affect your credit score. (This factor may determine as much as 15 percent of your credit score.)

6. Check your credit report and dispute any errors every year. Thanks to the Fair Accurate Credit Transaction Act passed by Congress, you're entitled to receive a free copy of your credit report. (See Appendix A for contact information.)

Action Application

Read Appendix A and request a copy of your current credit report. Identify errors, if any, and contact the three credit bureaus about them.

Consider going over your credit report with a financial adviser, so he or she can explain the report to you and help you resolve issues.

ACTION PLAN TO GET OUT OF DEBT

If you're like most Americans, you would probably agree that debt is a four-letter word. Blame our credit crisis on the culture. Blame it on the media. Blame it on our society that keeps saying, "Buy now…you deserve it…even if you can't afford it."

I regularly rip up credit card solicitations and mortgage company letters telling me to borrow up to 125 percent of our home's value. The Bible advises us that owing no one and living debt free is the ultimate goal. If we follow God's plan, He promises to make us the lender, not the borrower—the head, not the tail (Deuteronomy 28:12–13). That's what we're going for, right?

Some traditional financial planners will tell you to pay off all your debt before you ever think about investing. I don't think that's practical. If everyone tried to do that, most of us would never invest in anything.

Getting out of debt comes down to two things. First, good debt versus bad debt. And second, your needs versus your wants.

We all know what bad debt feels like. It's stressful, and it keeps you from sleeping at night. It's when you've used credit to buy stuff you really don't need or can't afford—clothes, vacations, stereos—and end up paying exorbitant interest rates for them. They say the first rule of holes is to stop digging! In order to start getting out of debt, you have to stop charging things you can't afford.

Not all debt, however, is bad. Financial guidance books such as *The Complete Idiot's Guide to Beating Debt* by Steven Strauss and Azriela Jaffe define the difference between good debt and bad debt. Strauss and Jaffe describe good debt as the debt that enriches your life. It could be a mortgage, which allows you to own your own home. Or a student loan that can buy you an education and help you plan for the future. Or a business loan that may help advance your entrepreneurial efforts.

Other authors, such as Robert Kiyosaki in *Rich Dad, Poor Dad*, are more stringent in their definitions. Kiyosaki defines assets as those things that put money in your pocket, which good debt often makes possible. For example, owning a small house or condominium which you rent out can be an asset and a good debt. Ideally you want the rent you charge to cover the mortgage payment for a positive cash flow at the end of the month. In this case, debt is being paid for by someone else and puts dollars in your pocketbook at the same time. It also represents something that you'll eventually own, debt free, and that will provide a source of passive income—money that you don't work for every month. Sounds nice as you enter your golden years, doesn't it? And it's not just nice—it's *possible*.

> Your ultimate goal is living debt-free.

Learning the difference between a need and a want will also help you reduce debt. I try to ask my children before we make any purchase for them, "Is this a need or a want?" Do we really need another Barbie doll that will end up at the bottom of a closet somewhere, usually naked? (Why is it Barbie dolls always end up naked?) Or is this something we actually need? (Like maybe some clothes for the Barbie dolls we have!)

Sometimes it's okay to buy or charge a want, as long as you actually have the money in the bank to afford it. But if you're in so much debt it looks like Jesus will come back before your balances are paid off, you should consider making purchases and charges *only* for your needs for a while.

While you reduce your debt, start considering your "fields." Assets and good debts make your money work for you and enrich your life. My husband and I were able to take our biggest asset and expense—our home—and use the equity in it to start our real estate business.

The key to getting out of debt isn't working harder, working more overtime, or getting two or three extra jobs for evenings and weekends. The key is *managing what you have in order to reduce debt, while buying assets.* Starting now!

For example, when buying our first investment home, my husband and I didn't have it all together. We weren't financial gurus, and we still had debt to pay off on a credit card. But we chose to invest in real estate, some of which doubled in value within two years. We could never have just saved that much money in that amount of time. Had we buried our talent in the sand and played it safe, we would still be in debt with no assets making money for us.

Are you still charging things you can't afford?

Contrary to what fearful thinkers would have you believe, it doesn't take much money to begin buying assets. Let's say you can save $1,000. (That alone might sound impossible—we'll talk more about it later.) What should you do with your $1,000? Should you take a vacation? Should you buy a new wardrobe? Maybe a down payment on a new car?

Sure, those things may enrich your life—but they won't make you any money. So what if you invested that money in beginning a small home-based business instead? From the money you make on your business, you might be able to pay off your credit card bills in full every month. Eventually you could invest in real estate.

Proven did this. She took the money she made from her home-based business and bought her field of dreams. Why can't we? And with the money you make from your business and real estate, you could take a much better vacation and start planning for your next one.

Do I have you dreaming yet? Are the wheels turning? It isn't just a dream. Just as I believe God wants you healthy physically, I believe He wants you healthy financially. And it gives Him joy to see you prosper. God will help you get out of this hole if you let Him. Stop digging, and start praying and thinking.

Action Application

Consider the following ten-point plan concerning your money. Don't be overwhelmed by it. Look it over, then prioritize your financial life and make your own list according to your convictions.

1. Pay God first. Set aside a certain amount of money every month as a tithe to Him. It's easy to become legalistic about the amount (for example, 10 percent), but I believe the percentage is between you

and God. Giving should be a source of delight for you because God loves a joyful giver.

2. Pay down your credit cards so your balance doesn't exceed 30 percent of your total available credit on each card. Begin with the card at the highest interest rate.

3. Now that your balance is below 30 percent on each credit card, begin paying these cards off in full, again starting with the card at the highest interest rate. This is important so you can start building wealth. If you have money in a savings account, earning maybe 4 percent interest, consider using that money to pay off the credit card with the highest interest rate first. Think about it: If you have a credit card charging you 17 percent while the bank is only paying you 4 percent on your investment, you're losing money every month.

4. After paying off your credit card debt (ah, won't that feel good!) keep only one or two accounts open, because having too many credit cards in your name can also impact your credit score.

5. Pass on the payment holiday. Many credit card companies and banks will offer you a break during the holidays by letting you skip a payment.

However, this will end up costing you more money by giving the credit card company full interest for an additional month. That keeps you in debt longer.

6. Make your credit cards pay *you* from now on. Use only cards that give you cash back, frequent flier miles, or some other end-of-the-year incentive. (We use a card that contributes a small percentage to our children's college education fund. As long as we're paying off the card's balance in full each month, that contribution is free money!)

> It doesn't take much money to begin buying assets.

7. Since you're paying God first and your credit cards are now paying you, begin paying yourself. Automatically deduct a certain amount from each paycheck to be deposited into a savings account (more on this later). I love direct deposit because I don't get the chance to change my mind. Do your best to forget about this money until you're ready to invest it. This kind of direct deposit needs to be separate from your company's 401(k) or 403(b) plan. (If your company offers such a plan and matches your contributions, by all means take advantage of that free money for your nest egg.)

8. Pay off your car and resist the urge to go buy a new one. Just like with your credit cards, not paying 10 percent on a car loan is as good as earning

10 percent. Unlike your mortgage interest, the interest paid on a car is not tax-deductible. One alternative to paying off credit card debt and your car loan is to borrow against the equity in your home. These types of loans are like huge credit cards you can draw on and pay back as often as you need to. Usually they carry much lower interest rates than credit cards and somewhat lower rates than car loans, and the interest you pay is tax-deductible. If you feel you have the discipline by now to wisely use a home equity loan, look for a lender offering "no points" and low up-front fees. (Each point represents 1 percent of the loan, which is an extra cost to you. For example, one point on a $100,000 loan equals $1,000.)

Remember to customize this list according to your own convictions.

9. Use part of the extra money you now have to begin investing, as Proven would, and part to take a small vacation, paying cash. (By now you need one!) Occasional rewards will help motivate you to continue improving your financial situation.

10. Be thankful. Be grateful to God for all you have. Tell Him this every day, praising Him even through the hard times. Watch how He transforms your financial life.

Let those who favor my righteous cause and have pleasure in my uprightness shout for joy and be glad and say continually, Let the Lord be magnified, Who takes pleasure in the prosperity of His servant. (Psalm 35:27, AMP)

NO-BRAINER SAVINGS

How are you going to pay for that vacation? You're going to pay for it without even lifting a finger. Without even a thought. As you've been paying down your debt and increasing your credit score, you should have also been automatically depositing a small amount of your paycheck (between 1 and 10 percent) into a savings account and forgetting about it. See how that kind of saving can pay off?

It's easy to devour all we have, isn't it? We get our paychecks, then we spend it. But not anymore, because the Bible is clear that we aren't to be foolish with our resources.

If at this point you're feeling badly about spending everything you make, consider the time I received my paycheck and proceeded to lose it. No, I didn't go on some frenzied shopping spree or fly off to a tropical spa (it sounds good, though, doesn't it?). No, I really *lost* it. Where did I put that darn thing? It wasn't in my purse or in my desk. It wasn't in my car or my home. Yes, I did have another check printed up, but what a pain! That's when I became a huge fan of payroll direct deposit. If your company offers you this option, take it. And don't put everything you make into your checking account, because you'll spend it. Trust me, if it's there in front of your eyes, you'll spend it.

Not only should you have a small amount transferred directly into savings, another small portion should be directly deposited into your 401(k) or 403(b) retirement account, at least to the point that your company matches your contribution. Company matching is free money! I personally believe most baby boomers won't be able to live off their 401(k) during retirement. Consider what the volatility of the markets did to many of our elderly citizens' retirement nest eggs at the turn of the century. As long as a 401(k) isn't your only investment, free money is free money, and you should get all you can.

> It's so easy to devour all we have. But the Bible is clear that we're to steward our resources.

You say you can't afford to save anything? Yes, you can. Try. Your savings account will always be there if you need it. You won't be able to access your 401(k) account without penalties, but look at it as your savings account for when you're older. Take care of your older self now, while you can work, and make it all happen without a thought through direct deposit.

Action Application

Pay a visit to your company's human resources department this week to sign up for direct deposit. Make sure a percentage of your check goes directly into savings.

In the house of the wise are stores of choice food and oil,
but a foolish man devours all he has. (Proverbs 21:20, NIV)

THE POWER OF COMPOUNDING

If paper assets are your field of investment, realize that compounding is a wonderful thing. In *Every Woman's Guide to Financial Security*, authors Ann Peterson and Stephen Rosenberg tell the story of a woman named Belinda whose husband passed away while she was still a young woman. She received $50,000 in insurance proceeds and took the safe path by investing in certificates of deposit at her local bank. The bank, in turn, deposited the interest from that CD into her savings account, which she could withdraw from anytime she wanted. At 8.7 percent interest, her original investment of $50,000 is still $50,000 today because all the interest went to her savings account and not to her investment. Had she chosen to reinvest her money over the twenty-six years that have followed, that investment would now be worth $437,460!

The power of compounding works because the money you save earns interest. Then you earn more interest on your original investment, plus the interest you've accumulated. As your savings grows, you continue to earn interest on a bigger investment, turning even small investments into larger accounts, given enough time.

Most of the money in this country is kept in banks and credit unions, which offer a good measure of safety and reliability if your tolerance for risk is low. This is also a better choice than burying your talents in the sand. Consider again the Parable of the Talents:

And the one also who had received the one talent came up and said, "Master, I knew you to be a hard man, reaping where you did not sow and gathering where you scattered no seed. And I was afraid, and went away and hid your talent in the ground. See, you have what is yours."

But his master answered and said to him, "You wicked, lazy slave, you knew that I reap where I did not sow and gather where I scattered no seed. Then you ought to have put my money in the bank, and on my arrival I would have received my money back with interest. Therefore take away the talent from him, and give it to the one who has the ten talents."

For to everyone who has, more shall be given, and he will have an abundance; but from the one who does not have, even what he does have shall be taken away. (Matthew 25:24–29)

Where can you allow the power of compounding to work for you?

While the master in this story mentions "the bank" as a safe solution, he's also unambiguous in rewarding the servant who took more initiative and had more risk tolerance. With your investments, if you want to play it safe, then at the very least use the power of compounding.

Another safe bet touted by many financial advisers is known as dollar cost averaging, where you invest the same dollar amount regularly in stocks or mutual funds. With this approach, you buy more shares when the price goes down and fewer shares when the price goes up, allowing you to accumulate money over time and reducing the risk of investing a large amount of money at the wrong time. But what if the stock you've been investing in for years and years was Enron? Or what if the market crashes just as you're planning your retirement party? That's the risk you take when you invest in someone else's company. A Proven strategy? You tell me.

Action Application

Now that you have a more solid handle on your numbers, consider what your Proven strategy might be for your life. Dream. Plan. Now, prepare to begin.

> Unless the LORD builds the house, they labor in vain who build it; unless the LORD guards the city, the watchman keeps awake in vain. (Psalm 127:1)

Part IV

PROVERBS 31 PURPOSE

CHAPTER SIX

Eight Reality Checks for Your Checkbook

Now that you're creating work according to your interests and talents, considering your financial choices, and taking steps—slowly and intelligently—toward investing, it's time to put your specific plan on paper.

In doing this you need to stay flexible and sensitive to the Lord's leading. Your plan for freedom and purpose won't work unless and until you commit your work to Him. "Unless the LORD builds the house, they labor in vain who build it" (Psalm 127:1). I wasted many years asking God to get on board with *my* plans, instead of working in the flow of His will. Take my word for it; it doesn't work.

Now's the time to make a new commitment to the Lord—or maybe your first commitment.

COMMIT IT ALL TO THE LORD

My prayer to invite Jesus to be Lord of my life was pretty simple. Something like, "Lord Jesus, I want to know You personally.

Thank You for dying on the cross for my sins. I open the door of my life to You and ask You to come in as my Savior and Lord. Take control of my life. Thank You for forgiving my sins and giving me eternal life. Make me the kind of person You want me to be."

We're still working on that last part, and I'll continue learning and growing my whole life. But you can hold on to the promise that once you invite Christ into your life, using your own words in your prayer, He promises to never leave you. "God has said, 'Never will I leave you; never will I forsake you'" (Hebrews 13:5, NIV). It's settled—now and for eternity. You'll be with Him forever.

Walking with God on a daily basis is another story. You'll be tempted, tested, and frustrated, and you'll have days when obedience to Him is the last thing on your mind. It takes a daily decision to commit our lives and our work to the Lord and to walk in His ways, but the benefits are incomparable:

> How blessed is the man who does not walk in the counsel of the wicked, nor stand in the path of sinners, nor sit in the seat of scoffers! But his delight is in the law of the LORD, and in His law he meditates day and night. He will be like a tree firmly planted by streams of water, which yields its fruit in its season and its leaf does not wither; and in whatever he does, he prospers. (Psalm 1:1–3)

Daily rewards for a daily decision!

Honestly, one of the hardest things to do is to truly commit our financial future to God. In *How to Manage Your Money*,

Larry Burkett writes that one way to apply God's principles to our money matters is through "Financial Breathing"—exhaling bad habits and inhaling good principles.[13] He says that first of all, we must daily acknowledge His ownership of our assets:

> Trust in the LORD with all your heart and do not lean on your own understanding. In all your ways acknowledge Him, and He will make your paths straight. (Proverbs 3:5–6)

Truly committing our financial future to God is one of the hardest things to do.

Next, we must accept God's answers and direction and breathe in His goodness and wisdom. Just as parents know what's best for their children, God knows and does what's best for us:

> If you then, being evil, know how to give good gifts to your children, how much more will your Father who is in heaven give what is good to those who ask Him! (Matthew 7:11)

Commit your work to the One who knows you and loves you more than anyone else. Don't be afraid; you're in strong and capable hands.

Action Application

How can you commit your work to the Lord today? What are His plans for your life? By now, you're getting closer to your answers, aren't you?

As you think about this, remember these commands from the Lord:

> "Do not store up for yourselves treasures on earth, where moth and rust destroy, and where thieves break in and steal. But store up for yourselves treasures in heaven, where neither moth nor rust destroys, and where thieves do not break in or steal." (Matthew 6:19–20)

BE GENEROUS, SOMEONE IS WATCHING

I remember sitting in church one Easter as the elders were passing around the offering plate. The woman sitting beside me only pretended to put money in the plate. She faked it, just went through the motions! At first I thought no one else saw it except me, but then I realized God had seen it too. God watches all of it, and shouldn't He be the only One who matters?

> And He sat down opposite the treasury, and began observing how the people were putting money into the treasury; and many rich people were putting in large sums. A poor widow came and put in two small copper coins, which amount to a cent. Calling His disciples to Him, He said to them, "Truly I say to you, this poor widow put in more than all the contributors to the treasury; for they all put in out of their surplus, but she, out of her poverty, put in all she owned, all she had to live on." (Mark 12:41–44)

I would have been tempted to feel superior to my miserly church neighbor had I not for years also cheated God. Like the multitude, I would contribute only from my surplus. Even when I finally got on board with giving to God financially— also known as tithing—it was far less than the 10 percent God suggested in the book of Malachi:

> "From the days of your fathers you have turned aside from My Laws and have not obeyed them. Return to Me, and I will return to you," says the Lord of All. "But you say, 'How are we to return?' Will a man rob God? Yet you are robbing Me! But you say, 'How have we robbed You?' You have not given Me the tenth part of what you receive and your gifts." (Malachi 3:7–8, NLV)

Ouch! At tax time, in reviewing my charitable giving, I would think, "That's it? I could have sworn I gave more than that!"

Not until I started taking this much more seriously did I finally experience the joy and true wealth that God offers to everyone who will step up to this plate when it comes to giving. I finally made the decision to give 10 percent out of my gross income, not my net income. This meant God got paid before Uncle Sam—and, most significantly, before me.

Jesus said it: "Give, and it will be given to you..." (Luke 6:38)

At the time I made this decision, I was making a fairly substantial salary, and the number terrified me. So much for standing firm on faith. To keep me on the straight and narrow, I even set up a separate account for God and used it for all my charitable giving.

You may have heard the following story before, but I'll tell it again: Just like everyone I know who has made this decision—yes, *everyone*—I was remarkably blessed by God. I actually had money left over after giving to God's work and paying my bills. I kept checking the account again and again to make sure I hadn't missed anything. I was giving more than I ever had, but I had more money left over. How was it possible? *Only through God.* Remember Proven: "She extends her hand to the poor, and she stretches out her hands to the needy" (Proverbs 31:20). Not only was the Proverbs 31 woman providing for her family, she was contributing to her community.

If you hope to be blessed in this world, you have to bless others. Jesus taught this principle:

> "Be rich in good works, ready to give, willing to share."
> (1 Timothy 6:18 NKJV)

Then the King will say to those on his right, "Come, you who are blessed by my Father; take your inheritance, the kingdom prepared for you since the creation of the world. For I was hungry and you gave me something to eat, I was thirsty and you gave me something to drink, I was a stranger and you invited me in, I needed clothes and you clothed me, I was sick and you looked after me, I was in prison and you came to visit me."

Then the righteous will answer him, "Lord, when did we see you hungry and feed you, or thirsty and give you something to drink? When did we see you a stranger and invite you in, or needing clothes and clothe you? When did we see you sick or in prison and go to visit you?"

The King will reply, "I tell you the truth, whatever you did for one of the least of these brothers of mine, you did for me."

Then he will say to those on his left, "Depart from me, you who are cursed, into the eternal fire prepared for the devil and his angels. For I was hungry and you gave me nothing to eat, I was thirsty and you gave me nothing to drink, I was a stranger and you did not invite me in, I needed clothes and you did not clothe me, I was sick and in prison and you did not look after me."

They also will answer, "Lord, when did we see you hungry or thirsty or a stranger or needing clothes or sick or in prison, and did not help you?"

He will reply, "I tell you the truth, whatever you did not do for one of the least of these, you did not do for me." (Matthew 25:34–46, NIV)

When you give to anyone, it's as if you're giving to Jesus Himself. That's the heart of giving financially to God. You may be able to fool everyone else, but not Him. When the Israelites wanted to know how they were dishonoring God, He told them (through Malachi) that they were cheating Him out of their finances—by bringing blind, crippled, and diseased livestock to sacrifice on His altar while holding back their best animals to receive top-dollar in the market (Malachi 1:7–8). Robbing God with your money deeply offends God, and it also robs you of the blessings He wants to bring into your life.

God wants our best, and He wants the best for us. Try it. I dare you. No, forget about me; *God* dares you! He dares you to trust

Him with your money and to honor Him with your wealth. I know this is tough, but this is one area where He actually tells us to test Him. Listen to His words (continuing in the book of Malachi):

> "Bring the tenth part into the store-house, so that there may be food in My house. Test Me in this," says the Lord of All. "See if I will not then open the windows of heaven and pour out good things for you until there is no more need." (Malachi 3:10, NLV)

Action Application

Test Him in this! Give to the Lord and see if He doesn't give back abundantly, beyond anything you might have expected or dreamed of for yourself. Then keep giving, even when you're tested (and you will be—but you'll also be victorious if you don't give up on giving).

> Honor the LORD from your wealth, and from the first of all your produce; so your barns will be filled with plenty, and your vats will overflow with new wine. (Proverbs 3:9–10)

HONEST MISTAKES

"An honest answer is like a warm hug" (Proverbs 24:26, The Message). Isn't that the truth?

Some Bible versions say an honest answer is like a kiss. Either way, I'll take it!

I love spending time with friends who are real, honest, down-to-earth people. My best friends don't put up any pretense or pretend to have all the answers, and that's so refreshing to me. God wants the same thing. He wants you to come before Him honestly to deal with your past and to plan for your future.

Plus, He already knows. He knows how you feel about life, relationships, and money. If you're frightened, God understands. He isn't here to judge you but to help you.

So we can acknowledge this with David:

Real. Honest. Down-to-earth. Do these terms describe the way in which you come before God?

> O LORD, you have searched me and you know me. You know when I sit and when I rise; you perceive my thoughts from afar. You discern my going out and my lying down; you are familiar with all my ways. Before a word is on my tongue you know it completely, O LORD. (Psalm 139:1–4, NIV)

You cannot hide from God, so why try anymore?

If you're a parent, you certainly understand this with your own children. You probably already know who spilled the Juicy Juice on your cream-colored carpet that you had steam cleaned just last week, but doesn't it make you happy when your little one will actually 'fess up to it?

God is your Father. He's Dad. So why not work with Him and let Him work through you? This will happen only if you're completely honest with Him. He deserves no less.

Tell him this, as David did:

> You deserve honesty from the heart; yes, utter sincerity and truthfulness. Oh, give me this wisdom. (Psalm 51:6, TLB)

And He will give you that wisdom!

In my most troublesome times, when I've been completely honest with God, He shows up. Most times it wasn't how I expected Him to; He shows up in *His* way, which is, of course, the right way.

If you're confused or angry about finances, tell the God of all resources. It may seem like the end of the world to you, but it's a simple math problem for Him. God is infinitely bigger than your money problems, and if you come before Him with an open and honest heart, He will never, ever let you down.

In working through this book, you've taken a long, honest look at your past priorities, accomplishments, successes, and failures. Now move on. Put your past behind you and get ready to smile at your future.

One of my favorite books in the Bible is Isaiah, in the Old Testament. If you believe God never speaks to you, just spend an hour in the book of Isaiah and you'll get an earful from God and new insight into His passion and personality. He so desperately loves us and wants to create new and beautiful lives for us:

> "Do not call to mind the former things, or ponder things of the past. Behold, I will do something new." (Isaiah 43:18–19)

You may be proud of many things in your life. Be grateful for those times. There may be just as many things that you would love to forget, things that still hold you back. Let them go now. Holding on to those things wastes your energy and hinders you from all the wonderful things God has planned for your future. He wants you to smile again. Because it's not only possible for Him to prosper you—to give you a future and a hope—it's His *plan*.

God has forgotten your sins and wiped your slate clean, if you've accepted Jesus.

> As far as the east is from the west, so far has He removed our transgressions from us. Just as a father has compassion on his children, so the LORD has compassion on those who fear Him. (Psalm 103:12–13)

The Lord loves you so intensely, fiercely, and enduringly. Receive Him, and He will wipe your slate clean.

> Therefore if anyone is in Christ, he is a new creature; the old things passed away; behold, new things have come. (2 Corinthians 5:17)

Action Application

Be honest about three events in your life that you need to put behind you, and write down your thoughts about them. Then tear up this piece of paper and flush it down the toilet, where it belongs!

Write down three events in your life that have brought you the greatest joy. Post it on your fridge! Thank God for these events, one more time.

And thank Him for His deliverance:

I waited patiently for the LORD; and He inclined to me and heard my cry. He brought me up out of the pit of destruction, out of the miry clay, and He set my feet upon a rock making my footsteps firm. (Psalm 40:1–2)

YOU CAN'T DO IT ALL

I think one of the reasons Proven was so happy is because she didn't try to do everything.

At first it looks like she *did* do everything, but look again. One of the reasons she accomplished a great deal is because she had help. She had maidens. Okay, don't go looking in the Yellow Pages under "Maidens-R-Us." It isn't there. I've looked (just kidding). But Maid-4-U, or some variation thereof, does exist.

Don't tune me out on this! I know this is where women begin to experience that internal dissonance because we mistakenly believe we're supposed to be everything to everybody. We're not supposed to ask for help—or even need it, right?

Wrong! God doesn't expect you to do everything. If you try to, you'll burn out. I challenge you to find a place in the Bible where it says, or even hints, that God expects a woman (or a man) to do *everything*.

Let's listen to the advice Moses received when he was feeling overwhelmed:

Where in your life should you be asking for help? And who should you ask?

The next day Moses sat as usual to hear the people's complaints against each other, from morning to evening. When Moses' father-in-law saw how much time this was taking, he said, "Why are you trying to do all this alone, with people standing here all day long to get your help?"

"Well, because the people come to me with their disputes, to ask for God's decisions," Moses told him. "I am their judge, deciding who is right and who is wrong, and instructing them in God's ways. I apply the laws of God to their particular disputes."

"It is not right!" his father-in-law exclaimed. "You're going to wear yourself out—and if you do, what will happen to the people? Moses, this job is too heavy a burden for you to try to handle all by yourself. Now listen, and let me give you a word of advice, and God will bless you: Be these people's lawyer—their representative before God—bringing him their questions to decide; you will tell them his decisions, teaching them God's laws, and showing them the principles of godly living.

"Find some capable, godly, honest men who hate bribes, and appoint them as judges, one judge for each 1000 people; he in turn will have ten judges under him, each in charge of a hundred; and under each of them will be two judges, each responsible for the affairs of fifty people; and each of these will have five judges beneath him, each counseling ten persons. Let these men be responsible to serve the people with justice at all times. Anything that is too important or complicated can be brought to you. But the smaller matters they can take care of themselves. That way it will be easier for you because you will share the burden with them. If you follow this advice, and if the Lord agrees, you will be able to endure the pressures, and there will be peace and harmony in the camp."

Moses listened to his father-in-law's advice and followed this suggestion. (Exodus 18:13–24, TLB)

Moses listened to advice—and kept his sanity.

It's my opinion that you cannot have it all, at least not all at the same time. You also cannot *do* it all! I tried, and believe me, it doesn't work.

I'll never forget trying to nurse my second child while my first daughter—a toddler—clung to my legs wondering why she couldn't breast-feed too. All this while my stepson, God love him, who had just come to live with us full time, was parading his preteen friends around the house commenting on what a mess it was. I thought there was a good chance I would lose my mind. I was overwhelmed, and I began to get angry.

Before I catapulted into a full-fledged postpartum depression, I went to speak with a wonderful friend who simply said, "Carolyn, you need boundaries." The fact that I didn't know what she meant was a good indication of where my life was at the time. She recommended *Boundaries* by Henry Cloud and John Townsend, a lifesaver of a book that can help you determine what you will and won't do, what you can and can't handle, and how to get control of your life. It's all about where you draw the line.

If you're raising a family, it's okay to ask for help. It's okay to delegate chores and duties, even to your children. The responsibility at home will help them grow into responsible adults. It's okay to not be perfect. It's okay to capitalize on your strengths and the true desires of your heart. It's okay to strip things away:

> Since we have such a huge crowd of men of faith watching us from the grandstands, let us strip off anything that slows us down or holds us back, and especially those sins that wrap themselves so tightly around our feet and trip us up; and let us run with patience the particular race that God has set before us. (Hebrews 12:1, TLB)

Here's a thought: How about running just one race at a time?

Action Application

List the things that hinder you in your life. Then ask these questions about them:

- Where can I cut the fat?

- What can I delegate?

Take action and use wisdom to simplify and bring focus to your life. And remember these instructions and promises from Jesus:

> I tell you this: Do not worry about your life. Do not worry about what you are going to eat and drink. Do not worry about what you are going to wear. Is not life more important than food? Is not the body more important than clothes? Look at the birds in the sky.

They do not plant seeds. They do not gather grain. They do not put grain into a building to keep. Yet your Father in heaven feeds them! Are you not more important than the birds? Which of you can make himself a little taller by worrying? Why should you worry about clothes? Think how the flowers grow. They do not work or make cloth. But I tell you that Solomon in all his greatness was not dressed as well as one of these flowers. God clothes the grass of the field. It lives today and is burned in the stove tomorrow. How much more will He give you clothes? You have so little faith! Do not worry. Do not keep saying, "What will we eat?" or, "What will we drink?" or, "What will we wear?" The people who do not know God are looking for all these things. Your Father in heaven knows you need all these things. First of all, look for the holy nation of God. Be right with Him. All these other things will be given to you also. Do not worry about tomorrow. Tomorrow will have its own worries. The troubles we have in a day are enough for one day. (Matthew 6:25–34, NLV)

THE POWER OF NO

Do you believe being a "good Christian" means you should always say yes when requests are made?

Well, I've got news for you. Not only is that not biblical, it's also not economical. If you always say yes to everyone who asks, you'll end up resenting them and disliking yourself.

When I interviewed Dr. Henry Cloud, coauthor of the

book *Boundaries*, he reminded me that being a good steward of your life is in no way being selfish, because our lives are a gift from God. Just as a store manager takes good care of a shop for the owner, we're to do the same with our souls—and, I might add, our money.

Our growth is God's "interest" on his investment in us. When we say no to people and things that hurt us or stretch us too thinly, we're protecting God's investment in us.

Let's practice: "Can you work overtime tonight? We really need you to be a team player."

All together now: "No!"

"Can you chair the school fund-raising committee this year because, you know, the children are relying on you?"

One more time: "No!" And don't feel obligated to always provide some excuse for saying no.

Learn to protect God's investment in you...by saying no to demands that stretch you too thinly.

So you think you're not quite ready for such an emphatic no? How about "Wait"? Or "Can I have some time to think about that?" Next time you're faced with a decision—any decision—resist the temptation to give an immediate response.

Remember the instruction that James gave us from God:

If any of you lacks wisdom, let him ask of God, who gives to all generously and without reproach, and it will be given to him. (James 1:5)

If you don't know what to do or you feel guilty about saying no right away, then ask God, be patient, and you'll get your answer.

This principle is so critical in the world of investing. You must learn to say no. You must learn to be patient.

You must also face the reality that not everyone is going to like you. Will everyone applaud you as you take your time making decisions? Of course not. Will your financial adviser or real estate agent love you if you flat-out say no to their advice just because it doesn't sit well with you? You know the answer. You may feel a little pull at your heart as you think about disappointing people, but now is the time to get over it.

Be careful what you say yes to. Learn to love saying no when the time calls for it.

Remember again how Proven, our Proverbs 31 woman, considered a field before she bought it. She didn't just buy it right after she saw it. I bet she said no to a couple of fields before she found her field of dreams.

But just think how contrary the principle of wise consideration is to our fast-paced world today. Haven't we all been tempted to dial the number on the TV screen for the latest money-making plan (with a 90-day money-back guarantee)? Or the newest weight loss program? (Dial now, and you'll receive this extra bonus kit FREE!)

The Bible says we shouldn't be conformed to the ways and temptations of this world, but instead we should let God transform us through His teachings (Romans 12:2). I was asked to join a group of real estate investors who stressed the importance of making fast decisions. Many market investors echo this buy-now-think-later approach. But I don't. And never have.

I can't tell you how many people have been aggravated with me because I say no to an investment that simply doesn't feel right. And if I feel I'm being pushed to make a fast decision before I'm completely comfortable with it, my answer is automatic: *No.*

If saying no is tough for me, waiting is harder. In making difficult decisions, I've found that the problem usually lies with my failure to listen, as opposed to the Lord not answering. When I jump into a decision without taking time to really hear the Lord, that's when I invariably make mistakes.

I've found a simple strategy that works in helping me simply wait and listen. If I'm unsure of something or which direction to take, I make it a rule to wait at least twenty-four hours before making my final decision. I might miss the deal of the decade, but I've found that a better deal will usually come along shortly. Waiting at least twenty-four hours gives me time to clear my head, get away from the emotions of the situation, and—most importantly—listen to the Lord.

> If it's something I'm unsure about…I make it a practice to wait at least twenty-four hours before deciding.

If I'm facing a decision, I usually ask the Lord for wisdom before I go to bed at night. By morning, I have the answer. God has given me the wisdom I need. Perhaps it was there all the time, but I just didn't perceive it. The quiet of the morning helps me to hear the Lord. Removing myself from the intensity of the decision allows me to gain a completely different perspective.

As I follow this approach, I'll sometimes even be aware of problems I didn't consciously notice at first. On some level, a spiritual level, I picked up what was wrong, but I couldn't put my finger on it until I asked for wisdom, waited, and listened.

So whether the answer is no or yes, God always delivers. Wait for God's still, calm voice to speak and your quieted, untroubled mind to hear it.

THE POWER OF YES

Now that you've defined what you will *not* do, it's time to put on paper what you *will* accomplish. Let's call this "the power of yes."

Some people call this goal-setting, a concept which used to stress me out. I felt that once I put my goals on paper, I had to accomplish them or I would be a failure.

I'm much kinder to myself now, and much more fluid and flexible in handling my goals—the things in life I've chosen to say yes to. Truly, many of the goals I had as a younger woman were flat-out wrong, not at all what God intended for my life. And many of the plans He had for me were far better than anything I might have dreamed up. So why write your goals at all? Because when they're realistic and flexible, they become an important part of planning for your future. Remember, if you aim at nothing, you'll surely hit it.

Another mistake I made in writing goals was expressing what I wanted out of life without stating how to get there. The how-to's are what get you somewhere—a good plan will slowly, eventually allow you to achieve the desires of your heart.

But the how-to's are difficult to craft. Proven had to spend time considering before she could act. She considered a field before she bought it. She looked for wool and flax to work with her hands. She planned for her children's future and did not have fear about it, for all her household were clothed with scarlet, the best material she could buy.

Planning doesn't just happen. It takes thought and time. It takes consideration.

For me, financial goals have been fun to list and shoot for.

> Your goals are the things you've chosen to say yes to. What are these for you?

I love the game of investing. But the arena of my health is a different story. When I was trying to lose weight, I kept failing miserably. Nothing seemed to work and I couldn't (or wouldn't) stick to any diet or exercise plan I tried. So instead of focusing on the seemingly unreachable goal, I focused on the step-by-step plan to get there.

First I prayed for God's help, and then I admitted to Him and to myself that I couldn't lose weight on my own. I needed direction and accountability to learn to live as a slim person again. That was humbling.

I also needed to face the reality that I wasn't sixteen anymore and I couldn't eat everything my kids were eating, at least not every day. (Let's be reasonable; you've got to have a Twinkie at least once a year.) So I put the goal on paper: 125 pounds.

I weighed 150 pounds at the time, and my goal seemed completely out of reach. But instead of focusing on what I couldn't do and feeling like a failure again, I wrote out a plan:

1. Pray.

2. Find help and accountability.

3. Begin a reasonable exercise plan that works with
   my schedule.

After many false starts and stumbles along the way, and by remaining flexible in the how-to's, I've reached my goal with a plan that works in my life.

Yes, as you set your goals and try to reach them, you'll be

discouraged at times. Yes, you may fail. But keep reworking and rewriting your plan until you reach your goal.

Action Application

Write one goal that you haven't been able to achieve. Just one. Something that matters to you deeply. The one area of your life that keeps bringing you down, whether it be health, relationships, or finances.

Now list three possible, flexible, realistic step-by-step plans to reach that goal.

And begin.

As you pursue this wise path, remember what God's Word says about wisdom:

> Long life is in her right hand; in her left hand are riches and honor. Her ways are pleasant ways and all her paths are peace. (Proverbs 3:16–17)

LOVE WHAT MONEY CAN DO, NOT MONEY ITSELF

We must remember that multiplying our money doesn't mean we're supposed to be focused on money, obsessed with money, or in a love affair with money.

A century ago, John D. Rockefeller was one of the wealthiest men on earth, but he reportedly said this: "I've made millions, but they brought me no real happiness. I'd barter them all for the days I sat on an office stool in Cleveland and counted myself rich on three dollars a week." Money itself will never bring us happiness.

You've probably heard the verse, "Money is the root of all evil," but that's a misquote of the Bible. Money isn't the problem; *loving* money is: "For the love of money is a root of all sorts of evil" (1 Timothy 6:10). When you love money just for money's sake, you're in big trouble. It's a never-ending thirst that can never be quenched. The Bible says:

> He who loves money will not be satisfied with money, nor he who loves abundance with its income. (Ecclesiastes 5:10)

Money itself must not be your goal.

Jesus also said, "It is easier for a camel to go through the eye of a needle than for a rich person to enter the kingdom" (Matthew 19:24, NCV). Again, that doesn't mean God wants you to be poor. In fact, He promises to prosper those who love and obey Him. But that statement from the Lord does indicate that money must not be a goal in and of itself. I believe Jesus is making a point about how our financial situation can affect our desire for God. Many rich people really are arrogant and proud and don't believe they need God, whereas many who are poor are more acutely and desperately aware of their daily need for God.

The truth is that most of us struggle to keep our finances in perspective. I saw a survey indicating that money is the leading cause of conflict for America's couples. It's the stuff we fight about—because we give it the wrong priority.

Money is important, but the Bible is clear that money cannot take first place in your life. If we're honest, that can be a real problem. Don't we spend a majority of our time in money-making activities? Don't we spend a good deal of effort thinking about how to advance our careers or bring more money into our homes? Don't we spend seventeen years or more in educational institutions, preparing for the work world so we can make good money?

And yet the Bible is straightforward:

Wisdom's words: "Riches and honor are with me, enduring wealth and righteousness." (Proverbs 8:18)

"Do not store up for yourselves treasures on earth, where moth and rust destroy, and where thieves break in and steal. But store up for yourselves treasures in heaven, where neither moth nor rust destroys, and where thieves do not break in or steal.... No one can serve two masters; for either he will hate the one and love the other, or he will be devoted to one and despise the other. You cannot serve God and wealth." (Matthew 6:19–20, 24)

More tough words. And these are words I have struggled with, because how could I be free to serve God if I constantly had to work for money? Money was taking priority over my time and my thoughts. And yet God wanted me to multiply it, not just ignore it or reject it. But Jesus reminds us to keep it in perspective. Money cannot be first on your priority list. That's *God's* position: "Seek first His kingdom and His righteousness" (Matthew 6:33). God is first. Always!

And there *are* ways to fulfill our responsibility to multiply our money and be financially free without letting money be the "treasure" that we place at the top of our priority list.

Our Proverbs 31 woman put money in its place: It was a priority, but not first priority. Proven prospered financially but didn't let it affect her heart or change her desperation for God. She put the Lord before everything. She respected Him and took action to care for her family in every way, including contributing financially. This right perspective allowed her to "sense that her gain was good" and to "smile at the future" without forgetting that her true spiritual riches were in God.

What has brought me the most joy financially is what God can accomplish through the right use of money. I've watched the church we attend become a blessing to many in the Virginia Beach community through the generous financial giving of many prosperous individuals. I'm stunned by what CBN has accomplished worldwide through the financial resources of thousands of people. That's when money can be a joy—when it's in correct relationship to God, submitted to His will.

Remember again these words from Jesus:

> "I tell you, use the riches of this world to help others. In that way, you will make friends for yourselves. Then when your riches are gone, you will be welcomed into your eternal home in heaven." (Luke 16:9, NIrV)

Action Application

As a means to an end, how can the gift of money change your family or community for the better?

What would you like to accomplish financially to change someone's life?

The blessing of the LORD brings wealth, and he adds no trouble to it. (Proverbs 10:22, NIV)

DON'T GET DISTRACTED

In many ways, through many circumstances, God is patient and persistent in showing me how easily I can become distracted. Worry sidelines me, and in the past, people have easily gotten me off track the moment I took my eyes off God.

For example, I love to do step classes at our local YMCA. It's a cardiovascular class requiring much concentration, not to mention coordination, to follow the teacher's routine.

One day, another lady came into this class late and set up her step in front of me. I allowed myself to get totally distracted by her, and I ended up completely out of step. It took me several minutes to get back into the rhythm of the class.

In the class on another day, an older man came into the room and began sifting through the equipment looking for weights. My attention went from the teacher to the intruder, and once again I was totally distracted, off beat, and off balance. Thankfully, God's message hit me instead of me hitting the floor: I suddenly realized God was even with me in step class, and He was trying to penetrate my thick skull by showing me how easily distractible I was. It wasn't the other people's fault; it was mine. With my attention off the teacher, I couldn't do anything.

In my mind, I said, "Okay, God, I think I get Your point. The next person who comes in won't throw me off balance, because I won't take my eyes off the teacher and let my concentration be broken."

Then another guy came into the room looking for weights. This time I kept my eyes looking ahead and my focus on the steps. By the grace of God, I wasn't distracted, I stayed in step, and He and I silently rejoiced together.

What a significant analogy for life. I started noticing when people and my own fears and worries were throwing me out of step with God's plan. It happened when I took my eyes off my supreme Teacher, God, and directed my focus elsewhere.

What distractions in your life should you be more aware of?

I began this book as a generic outline for a speech I intended to give for an investment firm. The manager was hoping to attract more female investors. The problem was, on the day I began putting the speech together, I couldn't write. Writer's block has never really been a problem for me; instead, I tend to babble incessantly and write too much, a lot of which has to be thrown away. But that day, I experienced writer's block.

So I did what I try to always do when I'm confused: I prayed. (I would save a lot of time and energy if I learned to pray more often *before* getting confused.) The answer I got was that God didn't want some generic, common investment speech or outline. He wanted His story told—part of which is Proverbs 31.

This caused me to worry (as is characteristic of me). In prayer I said, "God, this investment firm is going to hate this! It will never work for them." His response was, "No, it won't. But who are you working for anyway?" So I began to write about the Proverbs 31 investor. I wrote about Proven. And I was writing for my true Chief Executive Officer.

I was reminded again that His Word is alive and applicable

to today's world. If God has numbered the hairs on our heads, He certainly cares about our finances.

I never did give that speech. God prompted me to stay in step with His plan, and this time, I listened.

Action Application

Isolate whatever might be distracting you and causing you to veer off course. Do you have any worries that are keeping you from reaching your goals? Write them down.

When you see these things in black and white, do they seem as scary?

Now, how can you and God overcome them together?

Trust in the LORD with all your heart and do not lean on your own understanding. In all your ways acknowledge Him, and He will make your paths straight. (Proverbs 3:5–6)

SMILE AT YOUR FUTURE

Proven smiled at the future. She worked with her hands in delight. She sensed that her gain was good.

I get the feeling that Proven was having fun, don't you? This was clearly not a depressed or negative woman. She was a woman of forethought and action. She knew how to take care of her family and to plan for the future while reaping positive rewards in her life. Proven is the unambiguous example of reaping what we sow in action and attitude.

With her security first in God, Proven could smile at the future for many reasons, one of which was her planning for the future. She wasn't afraid of winter, because she'd prepared her household for it. She'd made the best clothing she could find for herself and her family.

Strength and dignity were also her clothing. She was able to smile at the future because she'd invested in a business—a vine-yard that would feed her children and her children's children long after she was gone.

She also laughed at the days to come, because she wouldn't let doubt creep into her plans. She trusted in God, who's bigger than any challenge, obstacle, or hardship she would encounter.

She smiled at the future because she was ready for it. Do you believe, now, that *you* are a Proverbs 31 woman?

I know now, from my own experiences as well as from reporting on hundreds of life stories over the years, that our atti-tude toward life will absolutely determine our outcome. If you believe you'll never be able to handle your financial life, you'll be right. If you believe handling money successfully just isn't in your gene pool, you're right. You're limited only by your beliefs!

Conversely, if you believe you can successfully take charge of your money...then you will.

> What do you expect from your future?

If you believe God requires us to be responsible with our money, then know also that He'll give you the resources and the wisdom to handle it. If God expects us to multiply our money (talents), then He'll show you how. Plus, God's provision will allow you to smile at the future and work with your hands in delight. The end result will be sensing that your gain is good. That's a promise—God's promise.

Let those who favor my righteous cause and have pleasure in my uprightness shout for joy and be glad and say continually, Let the Lord be magnified, Who takes pleasure in the prosperity of His servant. (Psalm 35:27, AMP)

God wants you to prosper and to be blessed in every area of your life so you can be a blessing to others. God has big-time plans for your life, if you're willing to get on board with them. You can't buy food for the hungry when you can't feed your own family. You can't give away what you don't have.

But believing God wants you well—in body, mind, soul, and pocketbook—takes a decision on your part. A choice to search for what is good. A decision to look for what is positive about you and your situation, according to the standards so graciously given to us in Scripture:

How can you become better prepared for your future?

Whatever is true, whatever is honorable, whatever is right, whatever is pure, whatever is lovely, whatever is of good repute, if there is any excellence and if anything worthy of praise, dwell on these things. (Philippians 4:8)

So here's a tough question: Are you ready for the future? And are you ready for your children's future, when someday you're no longer here?

These can be hard issues to face—but you don't have to be afraid anymore. Just like Proven, because of God and through God, you can laugh at the coming days. He will not leave or forsake you, and He also expects you to do your job.

Your job involves estate planning as soon as possible. You may say you have no estate to speak of, but if you follow the Proverbs 31 woman's plan to create, consider, and invest, it's just a matter of time before you do. (Again, language matters when it comes to estate planning, so I've put together a few important points to get you started in Appendix D. As you draft a will or make a decision on whether a trust is right for you and your family, you'll know a few basic terms to help you begin.)

Again, the advice of a wise, trusted professional will help finish this process for you. And once it's complete, you can smile. Smile at your future.

Action Application

- Begin compiling important papers and accounts that relate to your estate planning.

- Find a competent and trustworthy adviser by interviewing several. Remember to look for their fruit! What do they have to show for what they say?

- Draft a will, if you don't already have one, and make sure your beneficiary designations are up-to-date. (You can pass $600,000 to your heirs free of federal estate taxes, upon your death. Through proper planning, you can double this exemption to $1,200,000 if you're married.)

- Consider a living trust which can greatly reduce the cost of your estate taxes.

CHAPTER SEVEN

A Final Word

One day at CBN, the actor Stephen Baldwin was the speaker at our chapel service. He was in town to promote an edgy, modern evangelistic film he'd produced.

As he discussed the potential success for the project, he summed it up well: He said the Lord made it clear to him one day that it was *God's* success, not just Stevie B's. God reminded him that "just as quickly as I raised you up, I can take you down." Oh, how true!

If you place your trust in the Lord and hold fast to the promises in His Word, you'll succeed. If you turn your back on Him, you'll ultimately fail. Don't forget the Lord, and you'll prosper and be blessed in the work He has for you. And don't forget Him as you continue to experience success:

When you have eaten and are satisfied, praise the Lord your God. Praise him for the good land he has given you. Make sure you don't forget the Lord your God....
But remember the Lord your God. He gives you the ability to produce wealth. That shows he stands by the terms of his covenant. He promised it with an oath to

your people long ago. And he's still faithful to his covenant today. Don't forget the Lord your God.... If you do, you will certainly be destroyed. (Deuteronomy 8:10–11, 18–19, NIrV)

Nowhere does the Lord promise that we'll all be millionaires; we will succeed only according to His will for our lives. That's a sure thing.

And when the day comes that you're successful, when your life is cruising along beyond your loftiest expectations, don't ever disregard God. Praise Him and don't forget to thank Him—a failure which happens all too often:

While He was on the way to Jerusalem, He was passing between Samaria and Galilee. As He entered a village, ten leprous men who stood at a distance met Him; and they raised their voices, saying, "Jesus, Master, have mercy on us!"

When He saw them, He said to them, "Go and show yourselves to the priests." And as they were going, they were cleansed.

Now one of them, when he saw that he had been healed, turned back, glorifying God with a loud voice, and he fell on his face at His feet, giving thanks to Him. And he was a Samaritan.

Then Jesus answered and said, "Were there not ten cleansed? But the nine—where are they? Was no one found who returned to give glory to God, except this foreigner?" (Luke 17:11–18)

Can you believe it? Ten men healed of a horrible, skin-eating disease, and only one turned back to express gratitude.

Don't you just hate it when you take time to do something nice for someone and they don't even say thanks? If we're hurt by this, can you imagine how God feels as He reaches out His hands to us every day and we forget to thank Him?

With thanksgiving, bring your requests before God, and then you'll experience His peace. God loves a grateful heart. You might say it's hard to be thankful when you have nothing, but for just a moment, think about everything you *do* have. Do you have a roof over your head? That's more than some people. Do you have a mind full of creative ideas?

> "In everything give thanks; for this is God's will for you in Christ Jesus." (1 Thessalonians 5:18)

For everything created by God is good, and nothing is to be rejected if it is received with gratitude. (1 Timothy 4:4)

Learn to be that one person in ten who thinks enough of God to look to Him and say, "Thank You!"

Many of us turn to God in hard times, but learn to be one of those few who also turn to Him in prosperity and success.

Think about how He feels. Have you ever had a friend who only turned to you when he or she needed something? They called you at all hours of the day to talk about their problems but never had time for yours. They were concerned with receiving but not with giving. Don't be that kind of friend to God. He wants friends who are faithful in bad times and good. Don't forget.

Before Me there was no God formed, and there will be none after Me. I, even I, am the LORD, and there is no savior besides Me. It is I who have declared and saved and proclaimed, and there was no strange god among you; so you are My witnesses…and I am God. Even from eternity I am He. (Isaiah 43:10–13)

Action Application

Don't ever forget the Lord and His grace to you. And as you faithfully remember, you will know His blessing more than ever:

If you fully obey the LORD your God and carefully follow all his commands I give you today, the LORD your God will set you high above all the nations on earth. All these blessings will come upon you and accompany you if you obey the LORD your God:

How regularly are you remembering the Lord's grace and His amazing blessings to *you*?

You will be blessed in the city and blessed in the country.

The fruit of your womb will be blessed, and the crops of your land and the young of your livestock—the calves of your herds and the lambs of your flocks.

Your basket and your kneading trough will be blessed.

You will be blessed when you come in and blessed when you go out.

The LORD will grant that the enemies who rise up against you will be defeated before you. They will come at you from one direction but flee from you in seven.

The LORD will send a blessing on your barns and on everything you put your hand to. The LORD your God will bless you in the land he is giving you.

The LORD will establish you as his holy people, as he promised you on oath, if you keep the commands of the LORD your God and walk in his ways. Then all the peoples on earth will see that you are called by the name of the LORD, and they will fear you. The LORD will grant you abundant prosperity—in the fruit of your womb, the young of your livestock and the crops of your ground— in the land he swore to your forefathers to give you.

The LORD will open the heavens, the storehouse of his bounty, to send rain on your land in season and to bless all the work of your hands. You will lend to many nations but will borrow from none. The LORD will make you the head, not the tail. If you pay attention to the commands of the LORD your God that I give you this day and carefully follow them, you will always be at the top, never at the bottom. Do not turn aside from any of the commands I give you today, to the right or to the left, following other gods and serving them. (Deuteronomy 28:1–14, NIV)

ADDITIONAL
HELP

Winning the Credit Game

FICO scores were developed by Fair Isaac & Company, Inc., for each of the three credit "repositories," which include Equifax (whose score is known as Beacon), Experian (formerly TRW, whose score is called FICO), and TransUnion (whose score is called Empirica). These scores were designed to be used as a statistical means of assessing how likely it is that a borrower will pay back a loan, and the scores are based on the borrower's "credit file." The scores are *not* a measure of the person's income, bank account, assets, age, race, gender, religion, marital status, or employment status.

According to Fair Isaac, the actual predictive variables and percentages used in the scoring process are summarized as follows:

1. Previous Payment History: 35 percent

- Severity, recentness, and frequency of delinquencies (For example, a recent late payment on a mortgage can result in a 50-point loss in the credit score.)

- Collections, public records, judgments, and liens

Payment history on a person's file is supplied to the repositories by those who have granted credit to that person. This includes both currently open accounts and accounts that have been closed.

2. Outstanding Debt: 30 percent

- Relationship between total balances and credit limits (High credit limits show that a person could potentially go into that much more debt, thus making them a higher risk. Your credit balance should *not* exceed 34 percent of credit limit. Don't max out your credit cards.)

- The number of balances across all trade lines (Having multiple accounts open increases your credit limits and creates a higher risk.)

3. Credit History: 15 percent

- How long credit has been in use (The older an item of derogatory credit is, the less it reflects in your score.)

4. Pursuit of New Credit: 5 percent

- Number of inquiries

- The amount of time since the last inquiry, based on the most recent twelve months

- Number of new accounts opened in the past year

In recent years, the repositories have recognized that mortgages and automobile loans are aggressively shopped. Therefore, the credit score models have been changed so that multiple inquiries within a fourteen-day period are counted as one, although all the inquiries will show on the credit file. Inquiries that are not reflected in credit scores are those from account management/account review, promotional inquiries, potential employer inquiries, and medical/health inquiries.

5. Types of Credit in Use: 15 percent

- Types of credit include installment loans, revolving accounts (including overdraft protection), and debit accounts (Aim to have a healthy mix of credit.)

REASON CODES

Every credit score is accompanied by a maximum of four reason codes identifying the most significant reason for a consumer's failure to score higher. The first two reasons reflect 65 percent of the score.

These four reason codes are:

01 — Amount owed on accounts is too high

02 — Delinquency on accounts

09 — Too many accounts opened in last twelve months

19 — Too few accounts currently paid as agreed

COMMONLY ASKED QUESTIONS ABOUT CREDIT SCORES

Why didn't a credit file receive a score?

For a file to receive a score, a borrower must have the following conditions in his or her credit file:

- No "deceased" indicator on the credit file

- At least one undisputed trade line that has been updated in the last six months

- One trade line open at least six months

Why are there duplicate accounts on my credit report when it's obvious they're the same account?

This is not the repositories' fault. Usually it's due to how the creditor is reporting the information to each repository. Most of the time the account numbers are different to some degree, and therefore the models cannot recognize them as duplicates.

There's information on my credit file that doesn't belong to me. What should I do?

Sometimes there is information on the report that is not the consumer's (for example, a late payment is reported when the payment was not actually late). Anyone who sees what she believes to be erroneous information on her credit report should contact the repositories, report the apparent error, and have them investigate the information.

The Fair Credit Reporting Act (FCRA) allows the repositories "a reasonable amount of time," generally not to exceed thirty days, to investigate disputed items.

If a correction in the information cannot be verified, it will be suppressed from the credit file until the repositories hear back from the creditor. If the creditor believes that the debt is still outstanding, it will go back on the credit report.

How long does information remain on my credit file?

Payment in full does *not* remove a history of previously late payments.

Time periods are measured from the date shown in the "date of last activity" field in the credit file. This is the date a payment became past due or the date the borrower made the most recent payment.

The length of time that information remains on a person's credit file varies according to the type of information.

For credit accounts, the time period is generally ten years for accounts that have been paid as agreed. For accounts not paid as agreed, the time period is generally seven years.

For collection accounts, information remains for seven years.

For courthouse records, information generally remains for seven years from the date filed, except judgments and collections.

Bankruptcy information generally remains for ten years.

Unpaid tax liens remain indefinitely. Paid tax liens remain for up to seven years from the date released.

If derogatory information is removed, how much will my score increase?

Removing or changing one specific derogatory item will not guarantee an increase in a credit score, because the score uses all the credit-related data and takes into account a number of compensating factors.

The older the derogatory information is, the less effect it has on the score.

Will debts shared with a spouse be removed from a person's credit file in the case of divorce?

A divorce decree does not supersede a person's original contract with the creditor. It does not release legal responsibility for any account. The creditor must agree to remove the joint partner.

How do I contact the repositories?

You may call, write, or order the initial credit file through each repository's website.

If you write, you need to include a payment of nine dollars along with your full name, Social Security number, current address plus previous addresses in the past five years, date of birth, signature, and contact telephone number.

Contact Information

For a free copy of your credit report, also known as a credit file disclosure, visit http://www.annualcreditreport.com. This site allows you one free report every twelve months from each of the nationwide consumer credit reporting companies. Be careful to spell the website name correctly, because many fraudulent websites with variations of this name have already been established.

To contact the repositories directly, use the following information:

Equifax Information Consumer Services, Inc.
Disclosure Department
PO Box 740241
Atlanta, GA 30374
1-800-997-2493
1-800-270-3435
http://www.equifax.com

TransUnion
PO Box 1000
Chester, PA 19022
1-800-888-4213
http://www.transunion.com

Experian
PO Box 2002
Allen, TX 75013
1-800-397-3742
http://www.experian.com

Contact Information to Report Fraudulent Use of Your Credit

Equifax Consumer Fraud Division: 888-766-0008

Experian's National Consumer Assistance:
888-397-3742

TransUnion Fraud Victim Assistance Department:
800-680-7289

Government agencies:

Federal Trade Commission (FTC): 877-438-4338
U.S. Postal Inspection Service: 800-275-8777
Social Security Administration: 800-772-1213

To report check fraud:

Check Rite: 800-766-2748
Chex Systems: 800-328-5121
NPC: 800-526-5380
Tele-Check: 800-366-2425

The Language of Real Estate

THE PEOPLE

buyer's broker: A broker who represents the buyer when entering a real estate transaction. Generally, the seller pays the broker's commission at the closing.

creditor: A lender to whom a debt is owed.

grantee: A person obtaining title to real property by deed. The purchaser to whom the grant is made.

grantor: One who conveys title to property by deed.

listing broker: A broker from the office which created the MLS listing on a property. The listing agent represents the seller.

mortgagee: A lender of money under the terms of a mortgage.

mortgagor: The borrower who pledges his or her property to assure performance in repaying the loan.

optionee: The person who has the legal right to purchase or not to purchase, through a contract, a property in the future.

optionor: The seller of a property who extends an option to someone else. If the optionee exercises the option, this person is legally bound by the contractual obligations. But if the option is not exercised, then the optionor is released from any obligations.

real estate agent: A salesperson associated with a broker, who acts on behalf of the broker.

Realtor: A broker who is a member of the National Association of Realtors, as well as state and local real estate boards.

tenant: A person having the temporary use and occupancy of real property owned by another.

THE PROCESS

acceleration clause: Also known as a due-on-sale clause, this provision in a loan agreement allows the lender to declare the entire debt due immediately if the borrower defaults. Also known as a call provision.

adjustable mortgage loans: Mortgage loans under which the interest rate is periodically adjusted to coincide with current rates. The amounts and times of adjustment are agreed to at the inception of the loan. Also called: adjustable rate loans, adjustable rate mortgages (ARMs), flexible rate loans, and variable rate loans.

after tax cash flow: Gross income minus operating expenses and debt service, plus or minus any tax savings or tax liability.

amortization: The reduction of debt in equal installments of principal and interest over a fixed term.

annual percentage rate (APR): The yearly interest percentage of a loan, as expressed by the total finance charge actually paid, including interest, loan fees, points.

annuity: A payment of equal installments paid periodically for a given number of periods.

appraisal: An estimate or opinion of the value of a piece of property as of a certain date.

appreciation: Growth in value.

assessment: A government's valuation of property for tax purposes.

"as is" clause: A provision in a deposit receipt stating that the buyer accepts the property in its present condition.

balance sheet: A financial statement showing assets, liabilities, and net worth.

balloon payment: A large final payment on a note.

blanket mortgage: One mortgage that covers several different parcels of real estate.

buydown: A payment to the lender from the seller, buyer, or third party (or some combination of these) that causes the lender to reduce the interest rate during the early years of the loan.

cap: In adjustable rate mortgages, the limit on how much the interest rate or monthly payment can change.

capital gains: The profits realized above adjusted cost basis on the sale of property.

cash flow: Effective gross income minus operating expenses and debt.

closing: The final procedure in which documents are executed and/or recorded and the sale (or loan) is completed.

closing statement: The statement which lists the financial settlement between buyer and seller and also the costs each must pay.

competitive or comparative market analysis (CMA): This is a comparison of homes similar to a seller's home in terms of size, features, and location that have sold recently or are on the market.

contingency: A stated event which must occur before a contract is binding. For example, a home sale may be contingent upon the buyer obtaining financing.

contract: A legal agreement entered by two or more parties which creates an agreement to do or not do something.

deposit: A portion of the down payment given by the buyer to the seller or escrow agent with a written offer to purchase. Shows good faith.

depreciation: Cost recovery. This is a provision of the tax law that allows the owner of real and personal property to recover the cost of that property over a period of time specified by law.

down payment: Cash portion of the purchase price paid by a buyer from his own funds, as opposed to the portion which is financed.

easement: An interest held by one party in the real property of another, giving that person the legal right to trespass on the other's property.

eminent domain: The power of the government to take private property for public use in return for fair compensation.

encumbrance: A limitation on the title to real property. For example, a mortgage or an easement.

escrow: A procedure in which a third party holds all funds and documents necessary to the sale, with instructions from both buyer and seller as to their use and disposition.

equity: The value of an interest a person holds over and above any mortgages or liens on the property.

fair market value: The appraised value of a property as compared with other property values on the market.

FHA loan: A loan insured by the Federal Housing Administration, a part of the Department of Housing and Urban Development. FHA insurance enables lenders to loan a very high percentage of the sale price.

foreclosure: When a lien holder causes property to be sold so that the unpaid lien can be satisfied from the sale proceeds.

graduated payment mortgage: A mortgage initially offering low monthly payments that increase at fixed intervals and at a predetermined rate.

hazard insurance: Otherwise known as homeowners' insurance. This is a usual requirement of a mortgage lender to protect against loss.

index or rate index: A measure of interest rate changes used to adjust the interest rate of an adjustable mortgage loan. Example: the change in U.S. Treasury securities with a one-year maturity, based upon their weekly average yield.

interest rate: An amount a borrower must repay in addition to the full amount of the loan. This is the premium the borrower pays for the use of the money.

joint tenancy: A joint estate whereby upon the death of one joint tenant, his or her interest will go to the surviving joint tenant or tenants.

lien: A legal claim or charge on property as security for payment of a debt or for the discharge of an obligation.

loan-to-value ratio: The ratio, expressed as a percentage, of the amount of a mortgage loan to the appraised value or selling price of the property.

margin: In adjustable mortgage loans, the number of percentage points the lender adds to the index rate to determine the new interest rate at each adjustment.

MLS: MLS stands for multiple listing service, by which member brokers cooperate in the sale of each other's listings. Sellers may choose not to allow their property into multiple listing, if they wish.

note: The legal evidence or documentation of debt.

PITI (principal, interest, taxes, and insurance): Used to indicate the four major items included in a monthly mortgage payment.

points: A fee charged by a lender as a service charge or as an amount needed to make the yield on a mortgage competitive with other types of investments. Each point represents one percent of the loan amount.

prime rate: The rate of interest charged by banks to their best corporate customers.

principal: Amount of debt, not including interest; the face value of a loan.

private mortgage insurance: Insurance issued by a private company against a loss by a lender in the event of default. Private mortgage insurance is generally required for conventional financing whenever less than 20 percent is put down.

second mortgage: A mortgage which ranks after the first mortgage lien in priority.

title insurance: Insurance against loss resulting from defects of title of public record.

unsecured line of credit: A credit line which does not require collateral.

VA loans: Loans partially guaranteed by the Veteran's Administration, enabling veterans to buy a home with little or no down payment.

zoning: The laws which regulate and control what a property may be used for.

The Language and Rules of the Market Game

STOCKS AND OPTIONS

A stock certificate represents ownership of a certain number of shares in a specified company.

Trading in stock options can be risky but can also earn you more per dollar invested. (Options are contracts through which a seller gives a buyer the right, but not the obligation, to buy or sell a specified number of shares at a predetermined price within a set time period. Options trading allows you to profit on changes in a stock's market price without ever having to actually put up the money to buy the stock. You do, however, pay a premium for the option.)

Investment advisers point out four main differences between stocks and options:

1. A buyer can hold common stocks indefinitely, whereas options have an expiration date.

2. Common stocks are issued in a fixed number by
   the issuing company, while there's no limit to the
   number of options that can be traded on an underlying stock. The number of options traded is based
   on how many investors are interested in trading
   the right to buy or sell that particular stock.
3. There are no physical certificates for stock options,
   as there are for common stocks.
4. Unlike stock ownership, owning an option does
   not confer voting rights, dividends, or ownership
   of any share of a company unless the option is
   exercised.

MARKET LANGUAGE

aggressive growth funds: Stock mutual funds that seek high
growth through aggressive investment strategies. These
funds generally buy stocks of emerging companies that
offer the potential for rapid growth.

all or none: This directs the broker to attempt to fill the entire
amount of the order or none of it during the time limit you
specify. This differs from "fill or kill" orders requiring
immediate execution.

ask: The lowest price at which someone is willing to sell a security.

assets: Any item of monetary value owned by an individual or
corporation.

bear market: A period during which security prices are generally falling.

bid: The highest price at which someone is willing to buy a security.

blue chip: Describes stocks of companies known for high quality management or products which have a long history of stable earnings and/or dividend growth.

bond: A long-term debt security of a government or a corporation with maturity of ten years or more from the issue date.

brokerage account: An account with a brokerage firm that holds your investments, which allows you to buy and sell securities.

bull market: A period during which security prices are generally rising.

buy: Indicates you want to purchase a security.

call option: Gives its buyer the right to buy one hundred shares of the underlying security at a fixed price before a specified expiration date. Call buyers hope the price of the stock will rise.

cash equivalents: Safe and highly liquid assets, these types of investments can easily be converted to cash. Cash equivalents include: Treasury bills (T-bills), money market funds, and short-term certificates of deposit (CD).

certificate of deposit (CD): A type of debt instrument offered by banks or savings and loans. Generally, a CD is issued for a specific dollar amount, for a specific period of time, at a preset, fixed interest rate. CDs are FDIC insured up to $100,000.

commissions: The fees paid for executing a trade.

common stock: Common stock is "ownership" or equity in a corporation. An owner of a company's common stock is considered to have an equity position in the corporate structure of that company.

compounding: The computation of interest paid, using the principal plus the previously earned interest. Compounding measures the growth of an investment when dividends or appreciation are reinvested.

day order: Automatically expires at the end of the day's standard market trading session if it is not filled.

defined benefit plan: A company retirement plan in which you expect to receive a fixed amount on a regular basis from your employer, i.e., a pension. The employer is responsible for investing.

defined contribution plan: A company retirement plan in which in some cases, such as a 401(k) or 403(b), the employee elects to defer salary into the plan and directs the investments of that deferral.

distributions: The income or capital gain made by a mutual fund that is paid to the fund's investors.

diversification: A portfolio strategy designed to spread risk by allocating assets among a variety of investments.

dividend: A distribution of company earnings to shareholders. Dividends are typically paid to you in cash or stock.

dollar cost averaging: A strategy of buying securities in fixed dollar amounts at scheduled intervals, with the goal being to lower the average cost per share over time. Dollar cost averaging does not ensure a profit and does not protect against loss in declining markets.

Dow Jones Industrial Average (DJIA): Measure of the combined performance of thirty blue-chip stocks traded on the

New York Stock Exchange (NYSE), considered the leaders of the market.

earnings: The amount of profit a company realizes over a given time period after all costs, expenses, and taxes have been paid.

earnings per share: A company's earnings, also known as net income or net profit, divided by the number of shares outstanding.

employee stock ownership plan: A trust set up by a corporation to allot some of its stock to its employees over time. Used as an employee incentive, the plan often provides tax benefits to the company. Also known as a stock purchase plan.

exchange: A marketplace or any organization that provides a venue for trading securities, options, futures, or commodities. Examples of exchanges: New York Stock Exchange (NYSE) or the American Stock Exchange (AMEX).

face value: The displayed value on a bond, also called principal or par value.

Federal Deposit Insurance Corporation (FDIC): A U.S. government agency that insures cash deposits, including certificates of deposit, that have been placed in member institutions. The basic insured amount for each depositor is capped at $100,000. The FDIC's mission is to maintain the stability of and public confidence in the U.S. banking system.

fill or kill: Instructions that your order must immediately be filled in its entirety or canceled.

index: A statistical composite that measures changes in the economy or financial markets. Some indexes are used as benchmarks against which economic or financial performance is measured.

index mutual funds: Mutual funds that seek to replicate the performance of established securities indices.

Individual Retirement Account (IRA): A tax-deferred retirement account for individuals, which allows them to earn potential income on their investments and defer the taxes until withdrawals begin.

international stock: The stock of a company that is based outside the United States.

Keogh: Tax-deferred, qualified retirement account for self-employed persons and employees of unincorporated businesses. Contributions and earnings are deductible from gross income and grow tax-deferred until withdrawn.

large-cap, mid-cap, and small-cap stocks: "Cap" is short for capitalization, referring to the market value of a company's stock. Generally, companies whose stock has a market value of over $10 billion are known as "large-cap"; they're typically well-established with solid histories of growth and dividend payments. "Mid-cap" generally refers to companies whose stock has a market value between $2 billion to $10 billion, while "small-cap" generally refers to a market value below $2 billion. Small-cap stock funds are subject to greater volatility than those in other asset categories.

leverage: The degree to which a company or individual is using borrowed money.

liabilities: The sum of all outstanding debts.

limit order: A request to buy or sell a security only at a price that you specify or better.

liquidity: The ability of an asset to quickly be converted into cash. Generally, the greater the number of potential buyers and sellers of a particular asset, the more liquid it is considered to be.

load: The sales charge that some fund companies include when you buy or sell their mutual funds. Some funds have a "front-end" load, meaning you pay the sales charge at the time of purchase. Some funds have a "back-end" load, meaning the sales charge is paid at the time of the sale.

maintenance call: A "call" for additional funds or acceptable collateral to be immediately deposited into your margin account.

margin: "Buying on margin" means buying securities with money borrowed from a broker or dealer. It allows you to buy certain securities using the assets in your account as collateral for the loan. Margin can also mean the amount of equity required to buy securities purchased on credit.

margin call: This generic term refers to both maintenance calls and "Regulation T" calls (also called Reg T or Fed calls). An investor who receives a margin call is required to deposit additional funds or securities in a margin account either because the equity in the account does not meet the minimum equity requirement or because additional securities have been purchased or sold short. See *sell short*.

money market account: A vehicle in which accumulated funds are invested in various short-term securities.

municipal bonds: A bond issued by a state, municipality, or revenue district.

mutual fund: An investment company that pools money from shareholders and invests in a variety of securities, including stocks, bonds, and money market instruments. A mutual fund stands ready to buy back (redeem) its shares at their current net asset value, which depends on the total market value of the fund's investment portfolio at the time of redemption. As open-end investments, most mutual funds continuously offer new shares to investors.

NASDAQ: National Association of Securities Dealer Automated Quotations system, designed to facilitate over-the-counter stock trading.

net income: For a business this is the total revenue minus total expenses, which is the same as its net profit or earnings.

no-load mutual fund: A mutual fund that has no sales charge when shares are bought or sold. Be careful, however, because other fees may be applied, such as a "transaction fee."

operating expenses: The business expenses that mutual fund companies pass on to shareholders, including management fees. These costs are paid from a fund's assets before earnings are distributed to shareholders.

performance: The results of an investment's activity over time. Past performance does not guarantee future performance.

portfolio: All the various investments held by an individual investor or organization.

position: Security holdings in an account or portfolio.

preferred stock: A class of stock that pays dividends at a specified rate and has preference over common stock in the payment of dividends and the liquidation of assets.

Preferred stockholders may also have different voting rights. Not all securities have preferred stocks.

price: The cost for a security.

price/earnings ratio: Price of a stock divided by earnings per share.

prospectus: A legal document offering securities or mutual fund shares for sale. When you invest in a mutual fund, the prospectus will provide valuable information about the specific goals, fees, and practices of the fund. Federal and state securities regulators require that the prospectus include the fund's investment objectives, policies and restrictions, fees and expenses, and how shares can be bought and sold. It should be read carefully.

put option: Gives the buyer the right to sell a number of shares of stock at a price until the option's expiration date. Put buyers hope the price of the stock will fall. Puts may also be purchased to protect an investment in case the price of the stock goes down.

quantity: The number of shares you want to buy, sell, or sell short.

quote: The current "spread" relating the bid and the ask for a security. The bid is the highest price at which someone is willing to buy a security. The ask is the lowest price at which someone is willing to sell a security.

reinvestment: Using earnings or distributions from an investment to purchase additional shares in that security, rather than taking them as cash.

risk: The possibility for loss of some or all of the money you invest. Also, the degree of probability for such a loss.

risk tolerance: The degree to which an investor can financially and emotionally withstand declines in the value of his or her investments.

rollover IRA: A tax-free transfer of assets from one qualified retirement plan to another.

Roth IRA: A type of Individual Retirement Account that allows retirement savings to grow tax-free. You pay taxes on contributions, but not on withdrawals subject to certain rules. To participate in a Roth IRA, taxpayers are subject to certain income limits.

S&P 500 (Standard & Poor's 500 Index): Considered to be a benchmark of the overall U.S. stock market. This index is comprised of 500 widely-held stocks representing industrial, transportation, utility, and financial companies, with a heavy emphasis on industrials.

secondary market: A market where investors buy securities from other investors, rather than from issuers.

Securities Exchange Commission (SEC): A government regulatory agency that oversees and enforces the securities laws of the United States, publishes rules and guidance for the securities industry, and provides investor education.

security: A stock, bond, or other investment instrument issued by a corporation, government, or organization that signifies an ownership position or creditor relationship.

sell: Indicates you already own a security and wish to transfer ownership in exchange for money.

sell short: Indicates a "sell short" order when you want to borrow stock and sell it, with the understanding that you must buy it back later, hopefully at a lower price, and return it. This is a method of profiting from a declining stock price.

share: A unit of ownership in a company, mutual fund, or limited partnership. Company shares are represented by a stock certificate that specifies the company and the shareholder and number of shares.

stock: A document that establishes proportionate company ownership represented as shares. Different types of stocks have different advantages and responsibilities associated with them. As a stock owner, you share in the profits and losses of a company.

stock dividends: A dividend paid in stock rather than cash.

stop order: This indicates a request to buy or sell at the market price, but only when the security trades at or past a price that you specify, called the stop price. Once the stock price moves to or beyond the stop price, your pending stop order becomes a market order which guarantees execution, but not price.

symbol: The unique one- to five-character designation used to identify a security for trading.

tax-deferred: A provision that allows taxes to be postponed until a later date. Generally this applies to investments in retirement plans, annuities, savings bonds, and employee stock option plans.

tax-exempt: Accounts or investments that generally are free from tax liability.

tick: A small price movement of a stock. Also, the direction the price moved on its last sale. For example, an up-tick means the last trade was at a higher price than the previous one.

ticker symbol: The unique one- to five-character designation used to identify a security for trading. This is another name for symbol.

trade confirmation: Written statement acknowledging a securities transaction and its details.

Treasury note: A mid-term debt security of the U.S. government, with maturities ranging from two to ten years, that pays a fixed rate of interest every six months and returns its face value at maturity.

volume: The daily number of shares traded in a security.

yield: The annual rate of return of an investment paid in dividends or interest, expressed as a percentage. For a mutual fund, the yield is the rate of return earned by the securities in the fund's portfolio, less the fund's expenses during a specified period. A fund's yield is expressed as a percentage of the maximum offering price per share on a specified date.

The Language of Estate Planning

THE PEOPLE

administrator: The person or entity appointed by the court to handle the affairs of a person who has died without leaving a will.

beneficiary: A person named in a will to receive certain property of the testator. May also be a person who receives assets, income, or benefits from the existence of a trust.

decedent: The person who has passed away.

executor or executrix: A person named in the decedent's will to serve as personal representative (an executor, administrator, or anyone else who is in charge of a decedent's property) in probating the decedent's estate. This designated person has the right to decline to serve as personal representative.

grantor: A person placing property in a trust.

heir: A person who is legally entitled to inherit part of an estate of another person's property upon their death.

sound mind: The testator possesses sound mind for the purposes of making a will if he or she understands the nature of the act of making a will, knows the extent, character, and disposition of the property subject to the will, and knows the natural objects of his or her bounty (for example, his or her heirs). Whether the testator was of sound mind is determined by the state of the testator's mind at the time the will or codicil is written and signed (executed).

tenants in common: A form of ownership in which two or more persons have an undivided interest in the asset, where the ownership shares are not required to be equal, and where ownership interests can be inherited.

testator: One who writes and signs a will.

trustee: The person or legal entity who receives property and places it in a trust and manages the trust for the benefit of the beneficiaries in ways consistent with the trust declaration and good business practices.

YOUR PROPERTY

assets: Things of value owned by a family, a person, or a business.

estate: Everything of value that a person owns while living or at the time of death.

fair market value: The market price for an asset that would be agreed upon by a willing buyer and seller.

fee simple ownership: Property ownership where one person or entity holds the entire ownership interest.

intangible property: Property that only represents real value such as bonds, stock certificates, promissory notes, bank accounts, certificates of deposit, contracts, and other such items.

liabilities: Everything owed to others by a family, person, or business.

tangible property: Personal or movable property (such as real estate) that has value of its own, not just a representation of real value. Other examples are machinery, business equipment, inventories, and furnishings.

undivided interest: The interest or right in a property owned by each joint tenant or tenant in common. Unless an agreement to the contrary exists, each tenant has equal right to use and enjoy the entire property. Each tenant is also entitled to an income share proportional to his or her ownership interest.

THE PROCESS

codicil: A supplement to a will that modifies provisions of an existing will.

corpus of a trust: Term used to designate the property placed in a trust. The trust holds title to all the property included in the corpus.

escheat: When there is no heir to property, the property is assigned to the state because there may be no verifiable legal owner.

estate tax: A tax placed on the net value of a decedent's estate at the time of death.

gift: A voluntary transfer of property for which nothing of value is received in return.

gifting: An estate planning tool. Gifts are made to intended successors of assets.

grantor: The person who places assets in a trust.

holographic will: A will hand-written by the testator. The signature of the testator can be but need not be witnessed.

inheritance tax: A tax levied by the county of residence of a person who inherits property.

intergenerational succession: Property is transferred from one generation to another.

intestate succession: The distribution of property to heirs upon the death of a person who owned the property but did not leave a valid will.

irrevocable trust: A trust that cannot be changed after it is established.

lateral succession: Property is transferred between members of the same generation.

letters of administration: Document issued by the probate court giving the administrator authority to administer the estate.

letters testamentary: Document issued by the probate court giving the executor authority to administer the estate under the provisions of the decedent's will.

living trust: A trust established during the lifetime of the grantor.

partition: The judicial separation of the respective interests in property of joint owners or tenants in common.

probate: A court procedure for settling the affairs of a decedent by formally proving the validity of a will and establishing the legal transfer of property to beneficiaries. Also, appointing an administrator to supervise the transfer of property, if there is no valid will.

revocable trust: A trust that can be changed after it has been established. Assets can be added or removed and the beneficiaries can be changed. This type of trust becomes irrevocable upon the death of the grantor.

succession: A term used to describe transfers of asset ownership.

tax basis: The owner's cost of an asset for income and tax purposes as determined under the IRS Code and regulations.

testamentary trust: A trust established after the death of the grantor under provisions of a grantor's will.

Acknowledgments

How do I begin to thank all the teachers who contributed to my theories and thinking over the years? Countless people have cheered me on in success and cried with me in failure.

First on my list is God, who really is my best friend as well as the Lord of all resources.

I also want to thank my husband, John, who has lived this financial journey with me as partner and encourager during my 4:00 a.m. writing sessions.

God also put three special people in my life who inspired this book: our daughters, Lindsay and Brooke, who are Proverbs 31 investors in training, and my stepson, Jack, who will someday be a financial genius.

Much appreciation goes to my agent, Wes Yoder of Ambassador Agency, for making this project a success. Many thanks to the wonderful team at Multnomah Publishers, including my editor, Thomas Womack; Don Jacobson; Tim Nafziger; Bonnie Johnson; Kimberly Brock; Penny Whipps; and Jodi Carlson, for believing in this book and keeping me laughing during the process.

I would like to thank the staff of *Living the Life* and all of my friends at the Christian Broadcasting Network for their love, prayers, and support.

Special thanks to fellow William and Mary alumnus Jacki Payne, who was the first to read and edit my rough draft.

To my own financial team—real estate attorney Kirk Levy, CPA Kimberly Painter, and mortgage vice president Kim Pate—this book never would have been written without the lessons I have learned from all of you.

A special acknowledgment goes to my pastor, Michael Simone, whose creative, down-to-earth approach to Christianity has changed my life.

Finally, I would like to thank my parents, whom I love with all of my heart and still look up to. My mom always told me that I could do anything I put my mind to, and I was silly enough to believe her.

And lastly, this caveat: This book is designed to provide general information on the subject of personal finance. However, because laws and practices on financial matters vary from state to state and are subject to change, and because each personal situation is different, the advice in this book should be tailored to your particular circumstances, and I encourage you to consult with a financial adviser regarding the specifics of your situation.

The information in this book is not intended to serve as legal advice related to individual situations. As the author, I've taken reasonable precautions in preparing the text, and I believe the facts presented here are accurate as of the date the book was written. However, neither I nor the publisher assume any responsibility for errors or omissions, and the author and publisher specifically disclaim any liability resulting from the use or application of the information contained in this book.

Sources Consulted

Amos, Wally. *Man with No Name: Turn Lemons into Lemonade.* Sound Horizons Audio-Video, 1995. Print edition: Aslan Pub., 1994.

Bond, Robert J., and Walt Huber. *California Real Estate Practice.* 3rd ed. Covina, Calif.: Educational Textbook Company, 1994.

Brown, Jeff. "Emotional Investing is the Path to Grief." *Virginian-Pilot*, 25 September 2004.

Bundesen, Lynn. *The Woman's Guide to the Bible.* New York: Crossroad Publishing Company, 1993.

Burkett, Larry. *How to Manage Your Money.* Chicago: Moody Press, 1982.

Bussing-Burks, Marie. *Profit from the Evening News.* Naperville, Ill.: Sourcebooks, 2001.

Cloud, Henry, and John Townsend. *Boundaries.* Grand Rapids, Mich.: Zondervan, 1992.

Cohen, Herb. *Negotiate This! By Caring, But Not T-H-A-T Much.* New York: Warner Books, 2003.

Cook, John. *The Book of Positive Quotations.* Minneapolis, Minn.: Fairview Press, 1997.

De Roos, Dolf. *Real Estate Riches.* New York: Warner Books, 2001.

Devine, William Francis Jr. *Women, Men and Money.* New York: Harmony Books, 1998.

Drake, Marsha. *The Proverbs 31 Lady and Other Impossible Dreams.* Minneapolis, Minn.: Bethany House Publishers, 1984.

Faerber, Esme. *The Personal Financial Calculator.* New York: McGraw Hill, 2003.

Jerry Fung. *Real Estate Principles.* San Jose, Calif.: Dynasty School, 1993–2002.

George, Elizabeth. *Beautiful in God's Eyes.* Eugene, Ore.: Harvest House Publishers, 1998.

Hayes, Christopher, and Kate Kelly. *Money Makeovers: How Women Can Control Their Financial Destiny.* New York: Doubleday, 1997.

Huber, Walter. *Financing California Real Estate.* 3rd ed. Covina, Calif.: Educational Textbook Company, 1995.

Huber, Walter, and William Pivar. *Real Estate Appraisal.* Covina, Calif.: Educational Textbook Company, 2001.

Huber, Walter, and Kim Tyler. *California Real Estate Law.* 3rd ed. Covina, Calif.: Educational Textbook Company, 2001.

Kiyosaki, Robert, and Sharon Lechter. *Cashflow Quadrant: Rich Dad's Guide to Financial Freedom.* New York: Warner Business Books, 2000.

Kiyosaki, Robert, and Sharon Lechter. *Rich Dad, Poor Dad.* New York: Warner Business Books, 2000.

Lechter, Michael A. *Protecting Your #1 Asset.* New York: Warner Books, 2001.

Marone, Nicky. *How to Mother a Successful Daughter.* New York: Three Rivers Press, 1998.

McGee, Robert S. *The Search for Significance.* LaHabra, Calif.: The Lockman Foundation, 1984.

McKay, Harvey. *Pushing the Envelope.* New York: Ballantine, 1999.

McLean, Andrew James, and Gary W. Eldred. *Investing in Real Estate.* 4th ed. Hoboken, N.J.: John Wiley & Sons, 1988.

Reid, E. R. *The Proverbs 31 Woman: A Study Aid.* Shippensburg, Pa.: Destiny Image Publishers, 1993.

Rider, Stuart Leland. *The Complete Idiot's Guide to Real Estate Investing.* Indianapolis: Alpha Books, 2003.

Robertson, Pat. *Secrets of Financial Prosperity.* Audiotape series. Virginia Beach, Va.: Christian Broadcasting Network, 2004.

Rosenberg, Stephen M., and Ann Z. Peterson. *Every Woman's Guide to Financial Security.* Franklin Lakes, N.J.: Career Press, 1997.

Sears, Barry, and Bill Lawren. *The Zone: A Dietary Road Map to Lose Weight Permanently, Reset Your Genetic Code, Prevent Disease, Achieve Maximum Physical Performance.* New York: Regan Books, 1995.

Sheets, Charleton. *How to Buy Your First Home or Investment Property with No Down Payment.* Burr Ridge, Ill.: Profession Education Institute, 1999.

Spangler, Ann, and Jean E. Syswerda. *Women of the Bible.* Grand Rapids, Mich.: Zondervan, 1999.

Tobias, Andrew. *The Only Investment Guide You'll Ever Need.* New York: Harcourt, 2002.

Tobias, Cynthia Ulrich. *Redefining the Strong-Willed Woman.* Grand Rapids, Mich.: Zondervan, 2002.

Notes

1. Robert S. McGee, *Search for Significance* (La Habra, Calif.: The Lockman Foundation, 1984), 18–19.

2. Robert Kiyosaki and Sharon Lechter, *Cashflow Quadrant: Rich Dad's Guide to Financial Freedom* (New York: Warner Business Books, 2000), 232.

3. Elizabeth George, *Beautiful in God's Eyes* (Eugene, Ore.: Harvest House Publishers, 1998), 94.

4. Andrew Tobias, *The Only Investment Guide You'll Ever Need* (New York: Harcourt, 2002), 6.

5. Herb Cohen, *Negotiate This! By Caring, But Not T-H-A-T Much* (New York: Warner Books, 2003), 40–42.

6. Eleanor R. Reid, *The Proverbs 31 Woman: A Study Aid* (Shippensburg, Pa.: Destiny Image Publishers, 1993), 43–47.

7. Michael A. Lechter, *Protecting Your #1 Asset: Creating Fortunes from Your Ideas* (New York: Warner Books, 2001), xxv.

8. Marie Bussing-Burks, *Profit from the Evening News* (Naperville, Ill.: Sourcebooks, 2001), 71–73.

9. For example, see Jeff Brown, "Emotional Investing Is the Path to Grief," *Virginian-Pilot*, 25 September 2004.

10. Harvey Mackay, *Pushing the Envelope* (New York: Ballantine, 1999), 253.

11. Andrew Tobias, *The Only Investment Guide You'll Ever Need* (New York: Harcourt, 2002), 165.

12. Steven D. Strauss and Azriela Jaffe Steven, *The Complete Idiot's Guide to Beating Debt* (Indianapolis: Alpha Books, 1999), 253.

13. Larry Burkett, *How to Manage Your Money* (Chicago: Moody Press, 1982), 51–59.